THE FLAT TAX

THE
FLAT TAX

*A Citizen's Guide to the Facts
on What It Will Do for
You, Your Country,
and Your Pocketbook*

HOUSE MAJORITY LEADER
DICK ARMEY

Fawcett Columbine • New York

A Fawcett Columbine Book
Published by Ballantine Books

http://www.randomhouse.com

ISBN: 0-449-91095-4

Manufactured in the United States of America

First Edition: March 1996

10 9 8 7 6 5 4 3 2 1

Contents

Acknowledgments

I must start by recognizing Alvin Rabushka and Robert Hall. They deserve credit for, among other things, biting their lips whenever they hear their brain child referred to as "the Armey-Shelby flat tax." I may have introduced the bill in Congress, but they were the geniuses who developed a practical and fair flat-tax plan. All Americans who love freedom and honesty in government owe them a great debt.

I'm grateful also to the many bright thinkers, activists, and scholars who offered me their advice and assistance as this project moved forward. There is no way I could name them all here, but when the flat tax becomes a reality, they will deserve much of the credit. The folks at Citizens for a Sound Economy deserve a special mention. They have performed outstanding service to the flat tax and the cause of limited government.

Someone once said, "Show me a self-made man and I'll show you poor workmanship." In my case, I owe thanks to the best staff in Congress. Those who have worked especially hard on the flat tax include the following:

• My top aides Kerry Knott and (until recently) Ed Gillespie. They understood the enormous appeal of tax reform and encouraged the flat-tax project from the start.

• Brian Gunderson, who ran my personal office when the flat tax was introduced and who has helped guide the project since. Brian devised much of the strategy that in two years has turned the flat tax from a nearly forgotten policy initiative into a national movement. (He also served after hours as the organizer of this book.)

• Paul Morrell who, since rejoining my staff in September, has worked nearly every day to advance the flat tax. He is a skilled advocate and a very trusted adviser.

But, I owe particular thanks to Andy Laperriere, the promising young economist on my staff who, more than anyone else, has lived and breathed the flat tax since 1993. Without Andy's economic insight and unwavering idealism, the flat tax would not be front and center on the national agenda today. (Let's just hope he doesn't take his charts and graphs on his honeymoon this fall.)

I would also like to thank the very talented Matthew Scully who in two short weeks helped me condense two years' worth of my thinking, writing, and speaking on the flat tax into this concise book.

Further thanks must go to the production staff at Ballantine, and in particular to the book's editor, Doug Grad, who always gave wise advice. Doug and the Ballantine staff saw the need for a citizen's guide to the flat tax and worked long hours and weekends to finish this book in record time. It was a pleasure working with them. I also deeply appreciate the assistance of Lynn Chu. No one could ask for a finer literary agent.

Finally, my special appreciation goes to my wife, Susan, who again supported me as I became immersed in a national issue that we both believe is vital to our children's future.

A Picture of Simplicity

Imagine it's five years from now and April 15 is closing in: tax time. In the mail you have received Form 1 from the Internal Revenue Service, your only contact with the IRS since last year. It looks like this:

Form 1 **ARMEY-SHELBY FLAT TAX FORM** 1998		
Your first name and initial — Last name	Your social security number	
Present home address	Spouse's social security number	
City, Town or Post Office Box, State and ZIP code	Your occupation	
	Spouse's occupation	
1. Wages, Salary, and Pensions..	1	
2. Personal Allowance..		
a. $22,700 for married filing jointly	2(a)	
b. $11,350 for single..	2(b)	
c. $14,850 for single head of household......................................	2(c)	
3. Number of dependents, not including spouse..................................	3	
4. Personal allowances for dependents (line 3 multiplied by $5300)..	4	
5. Total personal allowances (line 2 plus line 4)................................	5	
6. Taxable wages (line 1 less line 5, if positive, otherwise zero)........	6	
7. Tax (17% of line 6)..	7	
8. Tax already paid	8	
9. Tax due (line 7 less line 8, if positive)	9	
10. Refund due (line 8 less line 7, if positive)	10	

Ten lines. On top, you write your total income. Subtract your personal exemptions. Take 17 percent of the balance and write that number on the next line. That's your tax bill.

Make out the check, drop it in the mail. You are done with the IRS for the next twelve months.

You are fully awake; you did not dream this. Within five years this may come to pass. You and I—and every taxpayer in America—will be paying that 17 percent rate and spending all of ten minutes in the process.

For all its simplicity, the flat tax is the most powerful and liberating idea in American politics today.

You'll pay a flat, single-payer rate of 17 percent on personal and business income alike, with one personal exemption to make sure you can support your own family before paying a dime to the government. Everyone is treated the same.

No more favoritism toward some citizens and harassment of others. No more loopholes. No tax breaks for corporations. No tax shelters. No depreciation schedules. No tables. Nothing.

It is hard to imagine so sweeping and profound a reform—an entire nation awaking from a nightmare.

Gone will be all the tax lobbyists who today roam the halls of Congress in search of special favors. Under the flat tax, there will be no such thing as a special favor. All the tax lobbyists will have to return to worthier, more productive pursuits.

Gone, too, will be the tax lawyers. Their entire discipline—based on a needless maze of rules and complications that make the rest of us miserable—will suddenly be rendered irrelevant. Gone will be the 480 different tax forms, and the 280 forms that explain how to fill out the 480 forms!

Instead of mailing out eight billion pages of forms every year, the IRS will send each of us just one card—nothing more. The income tax code itself—the IRS's four volumes and the 6,439 pages of official interpretation, libraries full of tax regulations, tax textbooks, journals, case law—all gone.

No more abuse of honest citizens by their own government. Discussion of taxes is always crowded with statistics. But how do we measure the aggravation, anger, and humiliation visited upon Americans today by the bullying bureaucracy of the IRS?

Under a flat tax, power will shift back to the ordinary citizen. You pay your flat rate, and that's that. End of discussion. The folks at the IRS will return to their humble task as collectors of revenue. Once again they will act as servants of the people, and not our supervisors. The flat tax bets on the goodness of the American people, not the guile of the federal government.

In the working life of America, we now spend some 5.4 billion man-hours each year deciphering the tax code. That's more man-hours than it takes to build every car, van, and truck manufactured in America. Some $232 billion of our resources are squandered on needless paperwork just to meet the demands of the tax code. That comes to a hidden tax of $900 on every man, woman, and child in the country, or $3,600 for a family of four.

Under a flat tax, that time and energy will be put to more productive use. Think of the difference that can make in our economy! The possibilities are staggering. The American economy will once again reward risk-taking, ingenuity, thrift, and personal effort. Success will not be thwarted and punished, as under our "progressive" system, but encouraged for the good of all.

In Washington, a merciful silence will fall over the Capitol. No more phony class-war rhetoric about who is or is not paying "their fair share." Who's paying what will no longer be a mystery or source of suspicion, because we will all be paying equally. Whether you're IBM or a mom-and-pop hardware store; whether your last name is Rockefeller, Kennedy, Gates,

Smith, Jones, or Armey—you fill out the same form, live by the same rules, pay the same rate on your income.

Throughout the nation's capital, all the bureaucrats who have used the tax code as their blueprint for social engineering, for meting out rewards and punishments on private behavior, will sit quietly at their desks. America's economic decisions will be left to us, to the workers and earners and creators of wealth, the way it was always meant to be in the first place.

Taken together, it's a picture of beautiful simplicity, of democracy in action, of Americans regaining power and government regaining its bearings.

The Coming Flat Tax

The flat tax is *the* issue in American politics today. But we are at a critical stage in the debate. That's why I've written this book.

In my experience as sponsor of the flat-tax bill, most Americans are instinctively drawn to the idea. Poll after poll supports this. It's not a matter of ideology. It's not a matter of party affiliation. Republican, Democrat, or Independent, we just like it in principle because it's fair. It's simple. It's neutral. And it appeals to commonsense economics: Scrap the tax code, tax everyone the same, leave more money with the people who earn it, and not only will life be simpler but the economy will flourish.

The surest sign of the idea's power is the intensity of opposition to it from the political establishment. We're hearing the usual grave warnings that greet any serious attempt to reform the tax code and return power to the people. *A radical idea! Too risky! Irresponsible!* Politicians always attack whatever threatens them and their power.

I will not concern myself too much with the complaints of the establishment. For such people, every serious tax reform is radical and wildly irresponsible, marking the end of civilization as we know it. Frankly, their deepest fears about the flat tax are all true: It will take their power away. It will leave the politicians less money to dole out to favored constituents. It will in every way put a check on their ambition to run other people's lives.

I will try to answer the concerns of the average citizen who leans toward having the flat tax, but understandably worries how such sweeping reform will affect him or her. What about the mortgage deduction? How will the absence of the charitable deduction affect worthy causes that rely on it? What about the self-employed person who enjoys all manner of deductions and write-offs?

One of the deeper problems with our current tax code is that, even as it fleeces us clean, it has made us, in a sense, all dependents. It claims huge amounts of our income, but then holds out one slender lifeline like the mortgage deduction or some special tax break. Though we regard the current tax code as an abomination, this or that little provision manages to ensnare us. We pay our protection money, don't like it much, but after a while there's a certain familiar security to the whole arrangement.

As I'll explain throughout this book, under a flat tax we will not need such "favors" from the government. Because of the personal exemptions before the 17 percent rate kicks in, nearly everyone but those who employ teams of accountants to massage their tax bills will pay less.

Why will there be no mortgage deduction? Because you won't need one. Under a flat tax you will be keeping more of your own money in the first place, interest rates will fall, and in general the whole economy will be a more hospitable place.

By their very nature, tax breaks and deductions and allowances are things government "grants" us, and can therefore be taken away at will. And usually they are. Every deduction the government ever gave to taxpayers it has eventually either cut or taken away altogether. Or else, as with the personal exemption we all enjoy today, the deduction erodes through inflation.

In a world of deductions and breaks and loopholes, we are all hostages to political fortune, never knowing what government will do next. Often we hear politicians promising even more "generous" deductions, as if they were doing you some big favor by letting you keep more of your own money.

The flat tax offers a world not only of simplicity, but stability. We'll know what to expect. Our futures will not rest in the hands of grasping politicians or restless bureaucrats. We won't rely on the "generosity" of Washington, but on our own efforts, on the fruits of our own labor and industry. And just to make sure that the fixed rate will not soon rise, my flat-tax bill has a provision requiring a three-fifths majority in Congress to increase taxes.

Perhaps the strongest case for the flat tax is our experience with other efforts to reform the tax code. They have been futile attempts to fix something beyond repair, to fine-tune a complete monstrosity fated not for the garage but for the scrap yard.

For as long as I have been in Congress—eleven years now—debate over tax reform has always tiptoed around the main problem. Once or twice we seemed within range of serious tax reform. The 1986 tax reform act moved the top tax rate from 50 percent down to 28 percent.

But then—up went the rates again. Every debate since then has degenerated into a haggling over meaningless detail. The government definition of "reform" has, until recently, meant tinkering around the edges: a tax break here, a new deduction there, a few more "allowances." With the tax hike of 1993—the single greatest tax increase in American history—the tax reforms of the 1980s became a faint memory.

This, among many other things, has brought about a

deep disillusionment with government. Washington worries about this decline in public trust. That's the bureaucratic idea of a "crisis in confidence"—when the people have more faith in themselves than they have in government.

The real problem underlying our entire, massive tax code is that government has so little faith in the people. Government today takes nearly half the people's earnings away, and then expects us to say "thank you." With every dollar government takes from you, it is taking more of your own power, independence, and dignity. It is saying, "You can't be trusted to spend your own earnings wisely—we'll do it for you."

Our founders left behind more than a few warnings about this. It's a seldom-recalled fact that the Constitution itself, before the Sixteenth Amendment was adopted, forbade imposing a graduated income tax on the people.

"The genius of liberty," said Alexander Hamilton, "reprobates everything arbitrary or discretionary in taxation. It exacts that every man by a definite and general rule should know what proportion of his property the state demands. Whatever liberty we may boast in theory, it cannot exist in fact while [arbitrary] assessments continue."

"The moment you abandon the cardinal principle of exacting from all individuals the same proportion of their income or of their profits," wrote J. R. McCulloch in *Taxation and the Funding System* in 1885, "you are at a sea without a rudder or compass and there is no amount of injustice and folly you may not commit."

I think that's the feeling at the heart of the flat-tax movement—the sense that as a nation we have no compass, no direction, no fixed principles guiding our tax policy.

We simply pay whatever the government is able to extract from us at any given moment. Even if some of us are faring better under the current tax code than others, we all live under an arbitrary, capricious, ever-shifting set of rules devoid of any principle whatever.

In just the past eighteen months, since I first introduced the flat-tax bill, something has changed in American politics. Something big, profound, and I believe permanent.

Call it a revolution, call it an electoral.shift, call it a turn in the political cycle—call it whatever you want, but clearly the American people have had it with the tax system. No more tiptoeing around the problem. Today we are talking about massive tax reform. Yesterday's "cranks" are today's prophets.

As I write this, the flat tax is the burning issue of the 1996 presidential campaign. It has propelled Steve Forbes, the novice in the campaign who was brushed aside only months ago, into serious contention, and thrown his opponents into turmoil as they vie to come up with variations of their own flat tax. The major Republican candidates have embraced the flat tax in principle—though later we'll examine the labels on these plans a little more closely. In some cases, they are flat only in name, half measures that buy into the basic premises of our current system.

Meanwhile, some in Congress have rushed forward with flat-tax bills of their own. The Armey-Shelby plan, charge the Democrats, would increase the deficit, bankrupt the nation, and, well, lots of other bad things.

We'll have a good look at their dire warnings, as well as their own flat-tax plan. I'm flattered by their attempt, but in truth it's little more than a futile, last-ditch effort to sell us more big government under a flat-tax label. Along the way, we'll also consider other objections to the flat tax manufactured by Washington's ever-busy statistics industry. In Washington, as we will see, you can torture the data until it confesses to anything.

We can't say for sure how the flat-tax debate will all play out in the 1996 election. But one of Armey's Axioms applies here: Never put a good idea in harm's way. In other words, the flat tax cannot be tied to the fortunes of any one candidate or party. Part of its power lies in its appeal to people of all parties and income groups across America. The flat tax is an idea carried forward by its own merit, its grand simplicity, its deep appeal to common sense. The idea doesn't need candidates—candidates need it.

I have felt this electoral wave coming for some time. Last year I published a book called *The Freedom Revolution*. In it, I devoted just one chapter to the flat tax. But everywhere I went on my book tour, that's all people wanted to talk about. At town meetings in my home district in Texas, always the first question is about the flat tax. The meetings soon turn into flat-tax seminars, with others rising to ask about this or that detail of the plan.

A supporter from Wisconsin wrote me recently to say he was offering up novenas to Saint Jude—the patron saint of impossible situations—on behalf of my flat-tax bill. I'll take all the support I can find, but I'm not so sure the bill falls under Saint Jude's jurisdiction anymore. A few years ago, maybe. But today the idea is square at the center of public debate. There's a zeal, a conviction, a hope in the public's response unrivaled by any other issue. I recently opened a home page for the flat tax on the Internet (*http://www.house.gov/armey.flattax*).

That the tax code will fall now seems to me the most obvious thing in the world. Anyone who ever stopped to think about the federal tax code, stepped back and really surveyed it in all its wonder, knew it was only a matter of time before the taxpayers of America threw it off. Like those barrels of tea in Boston Harbor, the tax code has been piling up, year after year, a symbol of everything gone wrong in America, of arrogant rulers and lost freedom, just waiting for us pick the whole thing up and heave it away.

It has to happen. Free people can only put up with such laws for so long. At a certain point we have to decide if we are really free anymore, or whether we are slowly becoming a nation of servants to government.

Are you free if you have to work five, going on six months a year just to pay taxes? We work on average until mid-May of every year just to pay our taxes. We pay more in taxes at all levels than we pay to buy food, shelter, and clothing for our families. Stretch that out over the life of the average working parent, and we're talking about twenty years of labor just to pay taxes. Is that freedom?

Are you free if you're compelled to follow a maze of rules and regulations you can't even comprehend? If you live in fear of arbitrary rulings, summary judgments, and stiff penalties from your own government? If, as a hardworking, productive citizen, you find yourself answering to some unelected official at the IRS?

Are you free if you're toiling away in factory, plant, or office, forking over more than a third of your earnings while some other guy with ten times your income pays nothing? Even with his $0 tax bill, how free is the other guy as he cowers behind his tax shelters and high-priced accountants?

That's not my idea of freedom. It's not my idea of good government, either. The whole sorry system is wrong. It's unfair. It's too complex. It's demoralizing.

Those who think tax debates are driven only by self-interest, by money alone or personal advantage, seriously underrate their fellow Americans. The question is much bigger than that. It runs much deeper. People support the flat tax because it speaks to our basic sense of fairness, our longing for simplicity and honesty in government, and our self-respect as citizens in a free country.

Many of the thousands of letters I've received are like this one from a supporter in Washington, D.C.: "I only wish that more people could understand the untold amounts of money needlessly wasted in our overly complex tax and regulatory system. As I am a tax attorney with the Internal Revenue Service, I must make it clear that my views are personal and are my own."

"A quick calculation," reads a similar letter from California, "shows that I personally would pay more taxes under the 17 percent you propose, but I still would support the concept wholeheartedly. What I really hate are the days spent plowing through receipts . . . and 2:00 A.M. qualms about what the IRS could do to me in an audit if they so chose."

"Although I consider myself a Democrat," said another supporter from Iowa, "I agree with you 100 percent and support your idea. I do not see any other fair method of taxation. I believe the current system is entirely unjust. I cannot see the fairness in charging some people a certain tax percentage and others a higher percentage. I don't understand why there are so many deductions that only the elite can afford to take. Please continue your push."

"I am a corporate partner in a major New York City law firm," writes a man from Scotch Plains, New Jersey, "and although I suspect that the adoption of your proposal would have the effect of eliminating all or a substantial part of our tax department, I believe the benefits of a flat tax far outweigh this and other short-term detriments."

The current tax code is not just a burden upon our lives and menace to our peace of mind. It is not just divisive, with its different rates for different groups, playing Americans against one another. It's not just an inconvenience to us all, a needless distraction from our lives and livelihoods. It is not merely a vicious thicket of rules and regulations no one of us understands.

The deeper problem is that it goes against so much of what we believe, what our country stands for, our sense of what it means to be an American. As I was walking out of a hotel in Dallas recently, the fellow who parks cars came up to me and said, "Congressman, I love your flat tax. I love it because it treats everyone the same."

That gentleman expressed it all. He pinpointed something very profound, very American, in the flat tax. In America, we define fairness as treating everybody the same. Rich or poor, black or white, we're all equal.

You don't have to be any sort of prophet to believe that the American people will not stand for our present tax code forever. The question isn't just how we can live under these conditions, but how, as Americans, we can live with ourselves.

Today we're at the breaking point. Enough tinkering in Washington, enough timid measures—time for something radical. This is no way for free people to live.

Chapter 1

The Tax Snare: What's Wrong with the Tax System

Nobody understands the tax code, but everybody knows what's wrong with it:

• Laws should be simple and clear—especially tax laws, because they hit nearest to home. Our tax code is beyond the comprehension of mortals.

• Laws should be written for the good of all, with a view to what used to be called the common interest. Our tax code is a grab bag stuffed with political favors to narrow special interests, paid from the pockets of ordinary citizens.

• Laws should be fair and uniform. They should not be tailored to any one favored group of people. Our code is "graduated," meaning in theory that the rich pay more, and in practice that they graduate to more advanced methods of tax avoidance. (By relying on people who graduated from law school.)

• Laws should rest upon basic and enduring principles of justice—not rewritten every few years according to the power shifts of the day. Our tax laws are arbitrary and unpredictable.

On each count—clarity, fairness, uniformity, and justice—our tax code is a complete failure.

In fact, our tax laws are the exact opposite of each standard. If we set out to design the tax code that way, we could not have ended up with a system more unclear, unfair, inconsistent, or unjust.

In this and the next few chapters, let's examine the problems one by one.

Clarity: Decoding Our Tax Laws

"What I consider just as important as the flat rate," a doctor in Maryland wrote to me recently, "is the simplification of the paperwork. My income tax return, including informational returns (which probably serve no useful purpose to the IRS) amounts to more than one hundred (yes, more than *one hundred*) pages per year. What is even more annoying is the fact that if I prepare this monstrous return by myself I would spend 546 hours according to IRS guidelines each year on top of the thirty-plus percent tax I am paying."

Here we have a productive citizen—a country doctor doing just about the most important work a person can do. Doubtless he has some investments that account for extra income—and good for him! To become a doctor took a lot of work. A fair and rational tax system wouldn't punish that effort. It would make as few demands upon this person's time and energy as possible, leaving him to pursue his calling and enjoy its rewards.

Since doctors have better things to do—like tending to patients—than pore over stacks of receipts, instruction books, and tax forms, he delegates the job to an accountant at a cost of thousands of dollars. The doctor's job is to care for sick people. The accountant's job is to care for people suffering under a sickeningly complex tax system.

The same story is played out across America millions of

times every year—the story of hardworking people harassed by their government. It's been going on for so long that we almost take it for granted. It's a given, like the changing of the seasons, that every year, having labored to earn an honest living, we have to begin another battle just to keep a decent portion of what we've earned.

What makes the situation so amazing is that it serves the interests of no one—not the citizen, not the employer, not the customer, not the economy in general, not even the government.

There's something perverse and self-destructive about it even from the standpoint of the tax man. Even if the great goal is to raise more revenue for government, this is a foolish and ultimately futile way to do it. By diminishing the rewards of work, it destroys the incentive. By killing the incentive, it reduces earnings. Lower earnings mean less government revenue. Everybody, the tax man included, ends up the worse off.

Even if we grant that government is entitled to a third or more of our earnings—I don't, but let's assume it just for the sake of argument—why does the whole process have to be so complex? Why can't the government simply say, "You owe us X percent of your earnings," and leave it at that?

Even at the IRS, some people understand this. "My employer is the Internal Revenue Service and my occupation is tax collector," writes a Washingtonian. "Since you asked my advice, let me give it to you. You should pursue the tenets and elements of your Freedom and Fairness Restoration Act uncompromisingly, unapologetically, with a vengeance. . . . In fact, if it rendered me unemployed, I would think it a good thing."

"I am a volunteer income tax assister for the IRS," writes another fellow from Lancaster, Pennsylvania. "Each year I do many, many tax forms for the elderly and low-income people. It is a shame that the 'average' taxpayer cannot even figure his own taxes. They frequently mention the unfairness of it all, and they are right."

It's easy to knock around the folks at the IRS. But the truth is that our tax code is so bad, so convoluted, so grossly unfair, as to be apparent even to most of its enforcers.

The original federal income tax code of 1913 was only fourteen pages long, and only about 2 percent of Americans even had to file returns at all. Fourteen pages—and probably even that was too long. Today the code runs for thousands of pages. To carry out these Innumerable Commandments, the IRS sends out more than eight billion pages in forms and letters to taxpayers every year.

Think of it this way. If you laid all those sheets of wasted paper end to end, you'd have enough red tape to wrap around the Earth twenty-eight times. And I suppose if you included the paper used by our accountants, you'd have enough for a nice big bow.

You've probably heard such statistics before. But they never cease to amaze me. Here's another one for the environmentally conscious: To make all that paper for the IRS, an estimated 293,760 trees lost their lives. An entire forest! Every year! Twenty years ago Jimmy Carter called the tax code "a disgrace to the human race." It's a good guess the displaced wildlife community isn't very happy about it either.

How we ever allowed such a code to pile up over the years, I'll never fully understand. Just by its very nature, big government seeks to control and codify every little feature of life. The first casualties are simplicity and common sense. Try, for example, to guess who or what is being described in this fragment of the tax code:

> (A) IN GENERAL—the term . . . means, with respect to any taxpayer for any taxable year, an individual—

(i) who bears a relationship to the taxpayer described in subparagraph (B),

(ii) except as provided in subparagraph (B) (iii), who has the same principal place of abode as the taxpayer for more than one-half of such taxable year,

(iii) who meets the age requirements of subparagraph (C), and

(iv) with respect to whom the taxpayer meets the identification requirements of subparagraph (D).

The answer is—child. If you're a mom or dad, this is how the government officially defines your little bundle of joy. To find yourself described, see subparagraph (B)(iii).

For all the aggravation such labored complexity causes the taxpayer, in Washington, of course, it's often taken as a sign of sophistication and responsible government. The more detailed, intricate, and (that favorite government word) "comprehensive" the proposal, the more compelling the idea and the more brilliant the person who thought it up.

Think back to the health care plan offered us a few years ago. Declaring a "crisis" in health care, the president appointed a task force of experts to solve the problem. A year later the task force reported back. The plan, a bewildering mass of new rules and agencies and federal mandates, came to 1,363 pages—doorstop material. To this day no one can really explain how it would have worked. For a time, though, the big thinkers behind it were hailed for their brilliance and attention to detail.

By the same token, the flat tax is today dismissed by the establishment as if the very simplicity of the idea was some sort of obvious flaw. If it's that simple, *something* must be wrong.

The whole big government mentality reminds me of Rodney Dangerfield in the movie *Back to School*. His character, a rich businessman who goes back to finish his degree, does no work at all but employs teams of experts to write his term papers for him. In one scene, an expert brings him an inch-thick research paper. Rodney takes it, weighs it in his hands, and then gives it back to the guy: "Nah, feels like a B+—more graphs!"

In the flat-tax "code," don't expect to find many subparagraph (A)'s and (B)'s, clauses and subclauses and hundreds of more pages to explain what each one means. There will be just one postcard-sized form to fill out, ten lines in all, end of process. People have better things to do with their time and money than sit around filling out stacks of forms for bureaucratic taskmasters.

Critics of the flat tax say the plan is just an outburst of anger from the people against government. Well, they're partly right. That may even be one of the best arguments for it. For years the bureaucrats have been saying to us, "More forms! More money!" Under the flat tax, they are going to be severely disappointed.

The flat tax will be a different kind of law, leading us back to a different kind of America—the country described by T. Coleman Andrews, director of the IRS back in the 1950s: "We are not the bosses of taxpayers," he said. "They are ours."

Chapter 2

Undue Burden: Compliance Costs

The humiliation is bad enough. That's the personal cost of our current tax system. Harder to grasp are the costs to the entire economy. The numbers are definitive proof of Chief Justice John Marshall's remark long ago that "The power to tax is the power to destroy."

"My wife and I," writes a businessman in Florida, "run two small businesses (an S Corp and a C Corp). Last year, we spent days just pulling together tax materials ... and we spent a combined $5,100 to have our accountant *just prepare* our company and personal tax returns. No bookkeeping, accounting—*just preparation of our returns.* Because of government regulations and complicated laws regarding employees, withholding, payroll, etc., we have continuously avoided hiring people in favor of keeping small and simple. I know a lot of intelligent people who feel and do likewise. Isn't it a shame that our laws/lawmakers continue to pile on business taxes, killing the entrepreneurial spirit within so many of us?"

From Butler, Pennsylvania, comes another letter telling the same story. If it's hard to follow the writer's description of her paperwork, think what it must be like to actually do it:

"I support your efforts to implement a flat tax. I am one

who is overwhelmed by the existing senseless and onerous tax requirements. I compute and pay: FICA and state taxes withheld from my husband's employees each month; FICA, FUTA, state Pennsylvania Unemployment Comp, and local payroll taxes; estimated personal and estimated corporate reports and payments quarterly; and personal income (generally including Schedules A, B, C, D, E, SE, and Forms 4562 and 6252), corporate, business privilege, occupational privilege, wage and real estate tax forms and payments annually. Preparation of tax returns, associated bookkeeping, calculations, and correspondence (often resulting from IRS errors) together with development of investment/tax strategies are all burdensome and time-consuming.

"This is not without cost to government," she adds. "Wasted time results in unrealized income, against which there is no deduction."

The writer doesn't even mention what the family business *does*, and it seems as if they don't have much time to think about it themselves. The federal government has in effect placed huge liens on their time and energy. Like small business owners across America, they have two jobs: They process forms for and send checks to the government. In between, they run their business.

How much does it all cost? It's hard to put a price on squandered time, especially for an entire nation. But for starters, think of it this way.

Along the East Coast we recently had a gigantic snowstorm. Businesses were shut down for days. People couldn't go to work. Important meetings were delayed, factories were closed, economic transactions of every kind were frozen in place until the streets could be cleared and people could get moving again.

In the days afterward, business reporters and economists tried to put a dollar value on the lost time. No one could say for sure, but the estimates came to billions of dollars. For struggling small businesses, where every hour counts, the effects were especially hard.

Now think of the effects of tax compliance and the time and energy it claims. There is no difference, except that instead of being bogged down in snow and mud, people across America are mired in needless and stupid paperwork. The flat tax, ridding us of the entire tax code all at once, is the big plow coming to clear away that horrendous blizzard of paperwork and rules once and for all.

The best estimate of total compliance costs comes to us from economist James L. Payne. His comprehensive 1990 study was very measured and detailed, but bore out the urgent warning of another economist testifying before Congress a few years ago: "If an enemy power bent on destroying our nation were somehow given an opportunity to devise our tax code with a goal of sapping the nation of its economic vitality . . . it could do no better than adopt our current Internal Revenue Code."

Begin with the cost of maintaining the IRS itself. That's about $10 billion right there, just to keep these devoted public servants on the job. The IRS employs more than 136,000 people to enforce the tax code—or about one IRS employee for every 1,911 citizens.

Not surprisingly, the IRS has been mercifully spared from the downsizing and "reinvention" measures supposedly going on elsewhere in the federal government. The IRS budget doubled over the past decade and staffing increased by 20 percent.

Payne then calculated the time we spend as a nation meeting the demands of the IRS code. Using research done by the Arthur D. Little research team, he put the figure at 3.6 billion hours for businesses across America.

That's 3.6 billion hours doing government paperwork and *not* spent doing something productive. And that was just his estimate using 1985 numbers. Today it's undoubtedly much higher.

How about individuals dealing with their personal returns? Total man-hours nationwide: 1.8 billion. The grand total: 5.4 billion hours people across America spend contending with the intricacies of our tax code.

Play with that number a bit, and the results are even more depressing. The typical taxpayer works 1,844 hours per year. If we divide 5.4 billion by that number, we then get the number of our fellow human beings who, in effect, are working full-time on tax compliance. The total is *three million people*—or thirty-two times the number of IRS employees.

Next, Payne converted those man-hours into dollars. The typical accountant was pulling down $35.47 an hour. (That was the average pay at a major accounting firm in 1985.) At the same time the typical IRS employee was making $21.14 an hour. Taking the average of those two—$28.31—you had a fair estimate of the hourly cost of a typical tax preparer. Converted to 1990 dollars, that came to $232 billion (along with about $80 billion in incidental costs) just to pay tax preparers.

What it all amounted to, said Payne, was an unbearable "excess burden" above and beyond the money we pay directly to government. It's a punitive tax on productive behavior, amounting, said Payne, to a hidden tax of 33 percent added to ever dollar. This means that for each dollar collected by the government in taxes, society loses another thirty-three cents because of lost economic output.

After all, what does government do when it wants to discourage a particular activity—smoking and drinking, for example? It slaps a tax on tobacco and alcohol. We call such punitive levies "sin taxes." Compliance costs, amounting to all these hundreds of billions of dollars, are in effect a tax on productivity—a "virtue tax" sapping away the strength of our entire economy.

And this is just the accounting and paperwork. Throw in

the time wasted across our country in tax litigation, preparing for tax audits, the monumental measures we take in tax avoidance, and the total comes to around $618 billion. That's $618 *billion*—nearly half the tax revenue we collect today and twice the cost of running the Department of Defense. Sheer waste. Taxpayers lose it. It doesn't go into any productive enterprise. It doesn't create jobs for anyone except tax lawyers and accountants. The government doesn't get it. It's just gone.

For a generation or so, politicians have been vowing to "get America moving again!" Until recently it was just another cliché, signifying nothing, except maybe a new array of government programs and "investments." Very few of us are stirred anymore by these calls to action. To get America moving again, we need to throw aside the big obstruction in our way. What's holding us back is a roadblock called the tax code, full of senseless rules that punish effort, kill initiative, and smother creativity. Scrap the tax code, free the taxpayers, and we'll see America move forward as never before.

Chapter 3

The Invisible Foot of Government

"I once started with $1,500, a secondhand kitchen table, and a donated typewriter, and—in ten years—built a $20 million-a-year business," writes a man from Evergreen, Colorado. "But I walked away from all that about fourteen years ago. Too many taxes, too many rules and regulations, too many bureaucrats.

"Get your plan passed *intact*," he adds, "and hundreds of thousands of people like me will come out of the woodwork and create prosperity that the world only sees now in some Asian countries!"

It's a sad day when Americans have to point to faraway countries as examples of free enterprise and prosperity. Not too long ago, people in those countries pointed to us as the example. We were—and in some ways remain—the model of industry and achievement, of what free people can accomplish.

This man has captured not only the despair and outright disgust many Americans feel today toward their government, but the faith we still keep. We still have the ideas, still have the desire, the drive, the resources, the ambitions. Given the chance, we could do it again. What's lacking under the current tax system is the incentive.

My correspondent is relatively lucky; at least he can afford to retreat to quieter pastures. Most of America's entrepreneurs and small-business people have to press on, slogging through the tax bills, regulations, and paperwork, making the best of a bad situation.

I remember another fellow I met in Washington State who came up to express support for the flat tax. Years earlier, he told me, he'd begun an electrical contracting company. That was his dream—to create a business all his own, and someday turn it over to his children. The business was doing okay, but one day he and his wife laid all their tax bills out on the table, along with all their permit fees, all the regulation forms, and all the paperwork. Then and there they decided: enough.

He laid off all twenty-two employees and thereafter accepted only those jobs he could handle himself. The whole thing was too complicated, too costly, and just not worth it.

Such stories are so common we've grown used to hearing them. But what a terrible indictment of modern government! Whatever political party we belong to, clearly something is wrong with a system that leaves hard-working people with no other option but to quit.

Such people are, and will always be, the ones who keep the whole economy going. They create the jobs, make the products, provide the services, and come up with the ideas. Most everything in our economy, government revenues included, rides on their success.

The driving force in our economy is incentive, the knowledge that effort will be rewarded. Saving, in turn, provides the dollars needed for further investment. Those investments—a new computer, a new tractor, more training— raise output and allow higher wages.

In almost every way, our current tax system is hostile to

productive and hard-working Americans. Instead of encouraging saving, work, and risk-taking, our current system does the following:

• Punishes effort with ever-higher, level-thy-neighbor marginal tax rates. Who's going to put in overtime when the reward is entry into a higher tax bracket? Who's going to take risks when success is met with confiscatory tax rates?

• Not only taxes too much, but double taxes our savings and investments. The system thus discourages the investments in technology that increase production and raise take-home pay.

• Mires worker, employer, investor—most everybody— in needless accounting and paperwork. Across our economy, hundreds of billions of dollars are squandered either meeting the demands of government or trying to avoid them.

• *Dis*courages productive investments, and *en*courages unproductive ones—tax shelters of little or no real value to our economy.

Ask any worker today what he or she finds most frustrating about the system, and the answer will be that wages and standards of living seem to be stuck in place. The same amount of effort doesn't seem to bring the same amount of earnings.

The culprit is obvious. Americans are forced to labor under a tax burden that's too heavy, tax rates that are too high, and a tax code that punishes saving and investment.

Heavy Taxes

Millions of middle-class earners today pay a marginal rate of 28 percent or more. On top of that, they pay a 15-percent payroll tax (the 7.5 percent you see deducted on your paycheck, plus the 7.5 your employer pays the IRS instead of you). And on top of that, an average of 5 percent in state/local taxes.

The pie chart below gives us the exact breakdown in the average family's expenditures as of 1994:

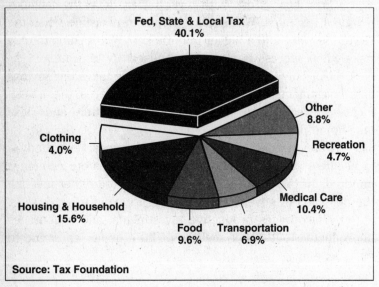

Expenses of a Typical Family 1994

In other words, just with the money they're able to earn, the typical family today pays more to government than they spend on food, clothing, and shelter combined.

High Tax Rates

The chart doesn't capture the disincentives people face to work harder and earn more. Most middle-class folks paying 28 percent, the marginal threshold, are taxed at 48 cents of every additional dollar earned. Who among us would feel much incentive to work harder, when nearly half our extra earnings go to the government? Who wants to put in overtime when every other hour on the clock is spent, in effect, in forced labor for the feds? That's the funny thing about progressive rates: the more we progress, the more we're punished.

Worst of all are the marginal rates imposed on the elderly. Having given them their Social Security benefits, the government now demands a portion of it back in taxes—a ridiculous situation that really amounts to a *cut* in benefits. These high marginal rates—reaching *82 percent*—provide the strongest possible incentive not to work even if they want to. Why should they work or contribute any further to our economy when every additional dollar is taxed at 82 cents?

Punishing Saving and Investment

Perhaps the most destructive feature of the current tax code is its bias against saving and investment. Under the code, income that is saved and invested is double taxed. Naturally, this discourages saving, which is why America's savings rate is among the lowest in the world. Because Americans save less, fewer dollars are available for investments in the new equipment and technology that raise worker productivity. Since wages only increase as workers become more productive, less saving directly translates into lower wages for American workers.

This is just common sense: When you have better equipment, you can be more productive and earn more. Why on earth then would we want to keep a code that violates this basic truth?

All these factors conspire to reduce our wages. The president's economic advisers were admitting as much in this passage from the 1995 *Economic Report of the President.* It's a little heavy with economists' jargon, but worth quoting because it lays out the basic numbers:

Growth in average real compensation declined from 3.0 percent a year between 1948 and 1973 to 0.7 percent a year between 1973 and 1993. This decline parallels a similar drop in worker productivity growth, from 2.5 percent a year to only 0.9 percent. If real compensation had continued to grow at the same rate after 1973 as it had in the previous 25 years, the average compensation of a full-time worker in the United States in 1993 would have been $62,400 instead of $40,000.

Given these burdens, it's pretty remarkable that our economy still grows at a rate of 2.4 percent a year. Today we hear from government economists that this is about the best we can hope for.

This is the same old big-government dogma we've been hearing for years: It assumes that taxes cannot be cut, that graduated rates are written in the stars, that government must ever and always sap away a trillion or more of our national wealth every year—that no fundamental changes can ever come about. I don't believe that for a moment. If we can manage a 2.5 percent rate under these tax burdens, just think what we could do without them. But doing that will require a new tax code.

Chapter 4

"Gucci Gulch": Fairness and Tax Breaks

For most people, fairness is not a complex idea. It means everybody gets treated the same. It means we're all held to the same standard—a fixed, clear, reasonable standard understood by all and, in a democracy, agreed to by a majority.

Our current tax laws show what happens when you abandon that simple notion of fairness. For starters, the targeted rich often avoid paying their higher rates through countless loopholes and deductions within the tax code itself. As a result, hundreds of billions of dollars in tax revenue are lost. Even by its own definition of fairness, progressive tax rates are a complete fraud.

Then there's the problem of lobbying. Since Congress has the power to grant special favors, our Capitol is the site of a continuing frenzy of lobbyists jostling each other for space at the trough. Lost in the whole sorry spectacle are the interests of the ordinary citizen, who has no bevy of lobbyists to do his or her bidding. I have never met a tax lobbyist who has a middle-income American for a client.

For the most part, the public interest lobbies are not much better. They claim to represent ordinary taxpayers but often make matters worse. For most of them, the public interest usually turns out to mean more government expenditures and, therefore, higher taxes.

And finally, even as government pampers some people under the current system with tax breaks and special favors, ordinary citizens find themselves harassed by an IRS that seems pushier and more arrogant every year, as the tax system grows more complex. Where did Leona Helmsley get the idea that "only the little people pay taxes"? From her tax accountants, no doubt.

Taken together, this is not my idea of a fair and just system of taxation. Even to call it a system or code at all is stretching things. It's not like Congress at some point gathered together America's best minds, charging them to devise the most enlightened and reasonable tax code known to man. The whole thing just piled up over the years, much as big government itself came together.

There was no grand design, no guiding principle, and no clear vision. Generations of politicians came and went and, with the usual mix of good intentions and radical irresponsibility, left us with this giant thing we call the tax code.

The fairness issue has to be seen from two angles. In this chapter we'll consider the influence of lobbyists over the tax code—the angle of the powerful. In the next we'll see how fair it looks to the largely powerless citizens, the great mass of Americans who cannot afford batteries of lobbyists to protect their interests.

Gucci Gulch

I'm always amazed at how often supporters of the flat tax mention the lobbying problem before they even complain about their high tax rates. There's something deeply troubling about it all, apart from the sheer cost to the taxpayer. It's just not the way things are supposed to work in a democracy.

Everybody knows this. Everybody bemoans the problem. But not a thing ever gets done about it.

"I am proud to consider myself a liberal," writes a supporter in Nevada, "and usually find myself diametrically opposed to your stands on the issues of the day. But you should know that I wholeheartedly support your efforts to move us to a flat tax with virtually no deductions. The current system is inherently corrupt. It is especially susceptible to the creation of special tax loopholes for big campaign contributors. This means that wealthy, well-connected Americans don't pay their fair share."

It would be a little misleading to say that most wealthy people don't pay their fair share. Even with their deductions and breaks and tax shelters, the wealthiest 5 percent of American taxpayers pay about 20 percent of all federal tax revenues. As we've seen in the case of businesspeople, the costs of compliance often rival the weight of the tax bill itself.

And—a point for another chapter—"wealthy" people whose income consists mostly of stock dividends and capital gains are actually paying a double tax today—once when the income is earned, and again when the money is distributed to them.

But the letter writer's general point is certainly on the mark: Our tax code is a standing invitation to corruption, preferential treatment, and influence peddling of every kind. Examine our tax laws, and you'll find hundreds of little items like this, a sample of "constituent services" as practiced today:

TAX EXEMPTIONS FOR CERTAIN OBLIGATIONS
FOR A PUBLIC UTILITY

(a) IN GENERAL—Subsections (b), (a), and (p) of section 103 of the Internal Revenue Code . . . shall not apply with respect to any obligation issued

after the date of the enactment of this Act with respect to a public utility facility if such facility is—
(1) located at any non-federally owned dam (or
on project waters or adjacent lands) located
wholly or partially in 3 counties, 2 of which are
contiguous to the third, where the rated capacity
of the hydroelectric generating facilities at 5 of
such dams on October 18, 1979, was more than
650 megawatts each. . . .

I'd tell you what all this meant—if I knew myself. This is
what's called a transition rule exempting one person or business from a tax, while throwing curious readers off the trail
with elaborate legal verbiage. Somewhere in the United States
is just one lucky utility ("utility facility") meeting this tortured
description. If that describes your business, then by the law
of the land you're off the hook.

The 1986 tax reform bill, which began as a genuine effort to reform the code, ended up with some seven hundred
of these tax breaks for deserving political supporters. Similarly, you got a tax break if you happened to be "a corporation incorporated on June 13, 1917, which has its principal
place of business in Bartlesville, Oklahoma" (Phillips Petro-
leum); if you owned "a stadium operating corporation with respect to which was incorporated on March 30, 1985" (I'd tell
you what company this is, but it's a mystery to me.); or "a
convention facility" whose "application for a state loan for
such facility was approved by the city council on March 4,
1985."

There are now some twenty thousand lobbyists in Washington whose sole mission in life is just to extract little favors
from Congress—at the expense of everyone else.

To most Americans, tax lobbyists are insidious but ab-
stract figures. You've read about the influence they have on
Congress. But like the Sasquatch said to roam somewhere in

the mountains of Washington State, you've never actually seen one.

Take my word for it: Their influence has been every bit as bad as you've heard—and then some. Since the 1994 election, things have gotten a little better. I don't want to sound partisan, but it's just a point of fact. With that election, Washington's tax lobbyists lost many an old friend and ally from forty years of one-party rule in Congress. But we still have a ways to go. Not until the tax code itself is abolished will the tax lobbyists be scattered once and for all.

In their excellent book on the 1986 tax reform debates in Congress, *Showdown at Gucci Gulch*, Jeffrey Birnbaum and Alan Murray paint the picture for us. It's the story of how the last great move for tax reform ended in a bill stuffed with even more tax breaks than before. Here they describe the scene in and outside of the Senate Finance Committee hearing room:

> Despite the late hour, the marble-lined committee room is packed to the doors with people, and guards are stationed at the entrance to stop more from pushing in. Deputy Treasury Secretary Richard Darman sits near the front of the room, facing the senators.... Surrounding him are the staffs of the Treasury Department, the congressional Joint Committee on Taxation, and the Finance Committee. Reporters sit cheek-by-jowl around two tables not far from the door, and the remainder of the room is filled with lobbyists—lots of lobbyists....
>
> In the hallway outside the committee room, more lobbyists stand nervously, like so many expectant fathers crowded into the waiting room of a maternity ward. The hallway loiterers include the top ranks of Washington's tax lobbying world—men

and women who are paid $200, $300, even $400 an hour to influence legislators and preserve tax benefits worth millions of dollars to their anxious clients. . . . A few of the lobbyists huddle around the back door of the committee room, hoping to catch a senator coming in or going out, hoping for one last chance to make their pitch before the vote. The desperation in their voices makes it clear that *big* money is at stake. The expensive suits and shiny Italian shoes give this hallway its nickname: Gucci Gulch.

The book goes on to detail all the other practices by which, as a matter of routine in Washington, democracy is subverted. For example, there is the influence of Political Action Committees—PACs. The authors note that from January to June of 1986—as the big "tax reform" debate was unfolding—contributions from PACs to House and Senate candidates went up 32 percent, from $50.7 million to $66.8 million.

In 1985—not even an election year—members of Congress who sat on tax-related committees received $19.8 million in campaign contributions. In the same year, the twenty senators on the Finance Committee netted a hefty $11.8 million in contributions. Members of the House Ways and Means Committee cleared a total of $8 million.

My favorite passages from *Showdown at Gucci Gulch* describe the state of affairs over in the House. At one time, of course, the big man in town was the chairman of the House Ways and Means Committee, Dan Rostenkowski. Hoping to take charge of the tax reform movement, Rostenkowski went on national TV and told viewers that if they had concerns about the tax code, they should just "write to Rosty." It was a populist appeal to ordinary Americans, inviting them to join the tax reform process.

The reality was quite different. In the book we read of

lavish fund-raisers held by the chairman with wall-to-wall tax lobbyists toasting the chairman. There were so many of these feasts, write the authors, that "staying slim was not an easy discipline to maintain. On one night alone in 1985, whole troops of lobbyists sped the half mile from a $500-a-head fund-raiser for John Duncan of Ways and Means to another $500-a-head event for Chairman Rostenkowski's PAC. In addition to shrimp, ice cream, and beer, those who attended the Rostenkowski fund-raiser received buttons that read: 'I Did Better than Write Rosty.'"

Here the author describes the chairman's philosophy of tax reform:

> In many ways, tax reform for him had become like any other tax bill. Deals had to be cut to keep the special interests from overwhelming the effort; votes had to be paid for with favors and special tax breaks. "I'm a negotiator," Rostenkowski said proudly. He built his bill by compromise, doing whatever was necessary to raise the revenue needed to pay for lower rates. He made no pretense to purity. "Tax reform," he said, "like all major changes in policy, is negotiated, not dictated. Like it or not tax reform ends up in a series of compromises. No compromise, no reform.... We may have to yield more to powerful interests."

I don't want to be too harsh here on Rostenkowski, who has since run into personal troubles, or on any of the others mentioned above. I'm sure that from their seats of power, all this seemed very reasonable. Enough power would do that to most of us.

In a way, the Rostenkowski credo is the best argument I've heard for abolishing our tax code in its entirety. On his own terms, he was right: So long as Congress is in the business of dispensing tax breaks and the like, so long as different groups are treated differently under the code, powerful interests will come knocking on congressional doors. Under such circumstances, tax reform is all but impossible. Between the faraway citizen and the lobbyist right here in Washington, with money to burn—the lobbyist will almost always win out.

Even today we still hear the lobbyists and their influence debated as if the whole problem were of some mysterious origin: How did all the lobbyists *get* here? As I write, various committees in Congress are having yet another go at campaign finance reform. But let's not agonize over it all too much. The problem is not that complicated.

It comes down to simple economic incentive: When you want a loan, you go to the bank. That's where the loans are available. When you want groceries, you go to a supermarket. That's where groceries are sold. And when you want a tax break, you go to the United States Capitol. That's where tax breaks came from.

Insidious as many lobbyists are, they are an entirely peripheral problem. They crowd the halls of Congress because our laws give them a powerful economic incentive to be there. Like ants at a picnic, they are operating by a perfectly rational calculation of self-interest.

The economist Friedrich Hayek explained this law of incentive years ago: "As the coercive power of the state will alone decide who is to have what, the only power worth having will be a share in the exercise of the power."

That's why, in the end, the flat tax is the only way of solving the problem once and for all. The trouble lies in the very idea of entrusting Congress with the power to tax people at different rates, instead of laying down one law for all. To abolish the code is a big step, but no bigger than the change that gave us progressive rates in the first place.

After all, for most of our history America was a flat-tax country. The progressive tax code has been around for most of *our* lifetimes, so we tend to take it as a given—as if the idea were etched on some sacred tablet. In fact, the first permanent income tax was only enacted in 1913. Progressive rates date back to just 1916.

Before that, few politicians ever dreamed of the powers exercised in Congress today over businesses, much less of taxing ordinary people at today's rates. The few who did were rebuffed by the Supreme Court, which held in repeated cases that graduated income tax rates were unconstitutional on their face. K Street in Washington—today the corridor of high-powered lobbying groups—back then was just a quaint little street with brownstone houses and corner stores.

There were the usual job seekers padding about our Capital. But if your business card said "Tax Lobbyist" or "Tax Lawyer," no one would have the foggiest notion of what you did, and probably you'd have met with a lot of suspicious looks.

By any sober reading of the document, the Constitution does prohibit tax favoritism of any kind. Section 8, Article 1 gives Congress the power to tax, but adds that all such taxes "shall be uniform throughout the United States." Reasonably enough, for most of our history most people, the courts included, took that to mean fixed rates, shared alike by all citizens.

"When the rule of arithmetical proportion is broken," warned one opponent of the idea, "the door is open to extortion." Without a fixed rate borne equally by all, Congress would inevitably abuse its taxing power, plundering some to buy favor with others. "When men get into the habit of helping themselves to the property of others," said a *New York Times* editorial in 1909, rejecting *any* kind of income tax, "they cannot easily be cured of it."

What's more, the idea of taxing different groups at different rates was, others pointed out, a variation on the "separate

39

but equal" doctrine. It divided Americans into groups, instead of viewing each citizen as an individual exactly equal in law.

That at least was the prevailing idea until 1916. For many of our troubles today we can thank the majority on the Court who, in that year, decided the case of *Knowlton v. Moore*. With that ruling, the principle of equality was abandoned and the Court put its imprimatur on the graduated rates.

Could politicians, the Rostys of that era, be counted on to tax wisely and with restraint? The Court dismissed such fears with this platitude:

> The grave consequences which it is asserted must arise in the future if the right to levy a progressive tax be recognized involves in its ultimate aspect the mere assertion that free and representative government is a failure, and that the grossest abuses of power are foreshadowed.

In other words, if Congress can't be trusted to use its taxing powers responsibly, then democracy itself can't be trusted.

In full agreement with this lofty sentiment, Congress quickly went to work plundering the national wealth: The top rate went up from 7 percent in 1916, to 14 percent in 1917, to 67 percent the next year, to 94 percent during World War II, leveling off to 91 percent until President Kennedy's tax cuts brought it down to 70 percent.

Back in 1916, the idea had been to get at the wealth of the "robber barons"—the Morgans and Vanderbilts and Rockefellers. But as with most tax laws, it all worked out a little differently. Inevitably, Congress took to broadening the definition of who was rich. Inevitably the rates of the middle class went up, too.

In 1930, the average American worker paid about 12 percent of his income to the government. By 1950, it was 25 percent. Today it's 36 percent.

With progressive rates, we stepped into the void, a tax system ultimately governed by no rule but raw political power. If Congress could freely confiscate the wealth of the rich, what could prevent it from confiscating more money from the almost rich, from the middle class, from anybody it thought needed taxing?

In effect, the progressive tax did not rid us of robber barons, but merely gave America a new set of robber barons: To pillage wealth and trample people's rights, from 1916 onward you first had to get elected to Congress. Originally based on "ability to pay," today our tax code is based on ability to pay off—to buy the favor of those in power.

That process ultimately led to today's hundreds of tax breaks, deductions, and loopholes. There was the mortgage deduction. Then a special break for farmers. Then the deduction for charitable contributions. Then an exemption for veterans' benefits. Then a deduction for certain investments. And so on until the present, when just about everybody—everybody but the working man and woman—has stock in the whole ludicrous enterprise.

What makes the problem worse is that many, perhaps even most, of these deductions are quite legitimate—if we accept the basic premise that Congress should be in the business of handing out rewards and punishments to a nation of supplicants.

On those terms it all makes perfect sense: If certain groups—homeowners, farmers, small business owners—cannot afford to pay their taxes, obviously they need a break.

But on those terms, even if we're getting one of those breaks, we're fated to live forever under a fundamentally corrupt and capricious tax system. To argue over the merits of each particular deduction is to miss the big point: A nation in need of hundreds of tax deductions and loopholes and breaks is an overtaxed nation.

"A simple, low, flat tax, together with limited government spending, and limited government regulation would sure produce a lot more prosperous Americans," writes a supporter from Middletown, Pennsylvania. "It would also remove a lot of the leverage that many politicians have over us. May God give us the courage to make it reality."

Right there is the key to it all—*leverage*. As long as government has power to treat taxpayers differently, it will have leverage over the people. Under the flat tax—one standard of fairness for all—the people regain their leverage over government. With the requirement in my bill of a three-fifths majority to raise the single rate—and with a little bit of that courage the writer mentions—maybe we'll never lose that leverage again.

Chapter 5

Middle America: Fairness and Main Street

"Since June 1995," writes a supporter from Texas, "my husband and I have spent two different days being audited for six hours. The reason for the audit was a computer error. The auditor quickly saw the mistake, but we continued with the frustration, humiliation, and lack of privacy and were treated as if we were dishonest. The reason I am writing to you is to encourage you to help eliminate the IRS and let the taxpayers go to a *flat tax*."

"It's about time," writes another supporter, "that the American people were relieved of that awful anxiety ritual perpetrated on them by the IRS. I am a senior citizen (a WWII veteran) who the president said when we were young we saved the world. I didn't save it for the IRS."

What the average citizen feels toward the IRS these days cannot be dismissed as the inevitable, age-old distrust between taxpayer and tax collector. It's much deeper than that. There's a profound sense of injustice about it all, and as much as anything, that conviction is driving the flat-tax movement.

The current tax code is inherently unfair, giving an edge to those with money and political connections. To those without such power, with no lobbyists and tax lawyers to buffer them from the IRS, it's worse than unfair: It's brutal.

I would guess that neither of these flat-tax supporters has all that much money. Very likely they're among those people who "work hard, pay their taxes, and play by the rules."

Nowadays that doesn't seem to matter much. You don't have to be a Wall Street high roller to attract the notice of the IRS. You don't have to wire large sums of money from bank to bank to come under suspicion. The only requirement for IRS attention today is that you (1) be a citizen of the United States, (2) work for a living, and (3) have at least a dollar to your name.

Let me be clear about one thing from the start. The good civil servants at the IRS are not to blame for this sorry state of affairs. They didn't write our crazy-quilt tax code, but they are duty bound to try their best to enforce it. It's an impossible task. But always remember—those who wrote the code and who fail to reform it are ultimately responsible for the heavy burdens placed on us by the tax collectors. If I had to police an incomprehensible tax code, I'd be cranky, too. My guess is that the folks at the IRS will be as happy as any of us when the flat tax finally comes to pass.

One hardly knows where to begin listing the aggressive tactics used today in the name of mere revenue collection. Aging veterans find themselves hounded over negligible amounts, hauled in for audits like criminal suspects. Senior citizens living on Social Security pay stiff penalties for the slightest mistake in their tax returns—a tax they're paying on entitlement benefits they supposedly have already paid for.

Waitresses subsisting on tips run into trouble for the slightest error on their returns. Small business owners—the people who create the ideas and jobs that keep our economy going—find themselves answering to an imperious bureaucracy. The IRS hands out fines and liens the way others hand out business cards.

Every year, in fact, a million and a half people face liens, often without warning. The IRS actually rewards agents based on their productivity in confiscating property. Like meter maids, they get paid according to each day's catch.

No doubt this helps explain why penalties imposed by the IRS have increased tenfold in the last fifteen years. In many cases, the money isn't even owed: According to the General Accounting Office, in 1990 the IRS imposed some fifty thousand incorrect, entirely unjustified penalties. The IRS now seizes the assets of three and a quarter million citizens, harassing four times more people than in 1980.

Without a warrant, the IRS can demand from banks, employers, and credit agencies virtually any information it wants. No other federal agency, including the FBI and Justice Department, has that sort of power. The IRS collects billions in penalties not even owed, merely because taxpayers are too intimidated to question the fine, or can't afford a tax lawyer to fend off the revenue sharks.

The IRS often intimidates businesses that hire out to independent contractors. It doesn't like the self-employed, of course, because their earnings cannot be withheld and in general they're just harder to watch. According to *The Wall Street Journal*, "Many IRS officials threaten harsh penalties to coerce businesses to sign agreements proposing not to use independent contractors." In return, the businesses receive the light treatment.

Just in case it might still be missing someone, the IRS today has some nine hundred "controlled informants" on the public payroll. Some are even accountants, paid to report on their own clients!

On top of all that, recently the IRS began carrying out an even more ambitious program called the Taxpayer Compliance Measurement Program. Each year, entirely at random, just by the luck of the draw, the IRS planned to "invite" 150,000 Americans to participate in the program by producing any and all documents for that year—including sworn affidavits—covering every last detail on their tax returns. The idea of the program, as IRS Commissioner Margaret Miller described it, is that the IRS will "audit the taxpayer, not just the tax return."

In other words, there need be no evidence of wrongdoing to prompt an audit, no cause for suspicion as in criminal cases. You're just called in on no grounds whatsoever and instructed to lay your life out on the table for official inspection. You're guilty until proven innocent. A doctor who survived one of these audits described the process as "an autopsy without the benefit of dying."

Meanwhile, the IRS's own financial affairs were found to be in a shambles in an audit by the General Accounting Office. The IRS "failed to account for 64 percent of the $6.4 billion it spent in 1992 for items such as office rental, salaries, and computers." Among other little oversights, the IRS couldn't confirm to the GAO whether it "actually holds some $797 million in assets it claimed it seized."

And then there are stories like this one I came across in a Heritage Foundation publication, quoting the magazine *Dollars & Sense*, a sure sign that things are really out of hand:

> Armed IRS agents seized Engleworld, an Allen Park, Michigan, day care center.... The seizure was carried out by the agency because Engleworld's owners owed the government more than $14,000 in back taxes, and has drawn fire from parents who maintain that they and their children were intimidated by IRS agents conducting the raid.... "It was like something out of a police state," recalled Sue Stoia, one of the parents. Stoia had gone to Engleworld to pick up her seven-year-

old daughter Catherine. Before they could leave with their children, parents say, they had to sign a form pledging to pay the government what they owed the day care center. "They indicated you could not take the child out of the building until you had settled your debt with the school, and you did that by signing a form to pay the IRS," Stoia explained. "What we were facing was a hostage type situation. They were using the children as collateral."

Similarly, there was the case of Paul Zwynenburg. His brother Mark was among those killed in the 1988 terrorist bombing of Pan Am Flight 103 over Lockerbie, Scotland. Within months of the tragedy he received this little condolence from the IRS: "In accordance with the provisions of the existing Internal Revenue laws, notice is hereby given that the determination of the estate tax liability discloses a deficiency of $6,484,339.39."

Pay up in ninety days, said the letter, or meet us in court. From news accounts, the IRS had learned that Paul was among other relatives of the victims suing Pan Am. But the suit had not even been settled. Amazingly enough, the IRS still dragged him into court, and the family had to hire a lawyer and accountant to fend off the tax bills.

On C-SPAN not long ago I heard one of the higher-ups at the IRS giving a speech. From the audience came some questions—direct but *very* politely phrased—about these rigorous methods. In each case, he acknowledged that the complaint was a common one, but pleasantly directed the questioner to take it up with Congress. He said the IRS is merely carrying out the will of Congress to the letter.

But the speaker made a valid point. The IRS as we know it today was in a sense inevitable. It's all of a piece with big government fed by an arcane tax system. There is no fair way

47

to enforce a fundamentally unfair tax code. There is no nice way to tax people at 30, 40, or 50 percent of their earnings.

Just as big government is impossible without a vast and coercive apparatus of tax collection, freedom is compromised with it. In the end every society has to make a choice: If you want to micromanage America with an intrusive tax code, you get the modern IRS. If you want freedom, you can get by with an IRS at a fraction of its current power.

"When we survey the wretched condition of man under systems of government," Alexander Hamilton wrote, "dragged from his home by one power, or driven by another, and impoverished by taxes more than by enemies, it becomes evident that those systems are bad, and that a general revolution in the principle and construction of Government is necessary."

That's what the flat-tax movement is all about—not just a reform but a revolution in principle, a reconstruction of an unfair system.

I always shake my head a little whenever I pass the IRS building in Washington. "Taxes," says the IRS's own credo, etched in stone over the building's entrance, "are the price we pay for civilized society."

Very few of us think of the IRS as a milestone on the road of civilization. In a civilized society, government does not tax people more than they can reasonably pay. In a civilized society, government agencies respect the rights of the people. In a civilized society, people are not hauled in at random to answer to government.

Above all, in a civilized society, the earners of wealth do not bow before mere collectors of wealth. Tax collectors, necessary as they are under any form of government, have very little to do with building civilization. More often they're the undoing of civilization. Great countries like ours are not built by officious bureaucrats, but by the labor and vision of free people left to use their own earnings as they see fit.

Chapter 6

The 17 Percent Solution

Just since 1950, there have been thirty-one "significant" reforms of our tax laws, plus another four hundred or so revisions to "fine-tune" the code. In the last few chapters we've seen the results: an irrational, abusive, and unbearable tax code not long for this world.

On one hand, we have too many Americans living under too many rules and paying too much in taxes. On the other, we have too many loopholes and tax breaks for a coddled class of congressional pets who pay little or no taxes. The tax system is beyond tinkering, beyond revision, rotten to the core.

The IRS is now 132 years old. I just hope they're not planning any celebrations to mark the big sesquicentennial. By the look of things, there's not going to be anything to mark, except the day when we abolish the tax code, level the IRS, and enact a single flat tax for all Americans.

Let's go back to the basic idea and how it would work. And here I should give credit where it's due. With Senator Richard Shelby of Alabama, I introduced the flat-tax bill before the House—the Freedom and Fairness Restoration Act. If it becomes law, as I believe it will, the taxpayers of America can thank Alvin Rabushka and Robert Hall of the Hoover Institution. They were advancing the idea years ago, back when I was still an economics professor at the University of North Texas watching Congress on C-SPAN. Come to think of it, Bill Buckley wrote a book twenty years ago called *Four Reforms*—his main reform being a flat tax—and before him there was economist Milton Friedman. Like most bold new ideas, I guess it's a lot bolder than it is new.

How the Plan Works

Because the flat tax is simple, it's simple to explain. The flat tax is a single tax designed to tax every dollar in the economy—once and only once. It's collected at two points: the individual and the business.

You've already seen the flat tax Form 1: all of ten lines. Individuals will add up their wage, salary, and pension income, subtract their sizable personal allowances, and pay a flat rate of 17 percent on the rest.

"I kept track last year as I prepared my return," wrote a woman from Colt's Neck, New Jersey. "It took me thirty-four and a half hours. And my financial life is not that complex: I'm retired, have a pension, and I own a few stocks and interest accounts. I tried filling out your 'Form 1.' It took me about five minutes."

That puts her a little ahead of the time I estimate it will take to fill out Form 1. The typical individual taxpayer today who handles his or her own filing spends an estimated eleven hours in the process. Under the flat tax, it will take no more than eleven minutes.

The tax for business is just as simple. Businesses would add up their receipts, subtract their expenses, and pay 17 percent on the rest.

That's it.

Tax Code Morality

What's important to understand is that the structure of the flat tax is not arbitrary. It's not something Rabushka and Hall or Dick Armey or Steve Forbes just dreamed up. There is nothing arbitrary in any of it. The whole design follows from a few basic principles, which I consider to be the basic principles of tax code morality.

- First, a fair tax system should have only one tax rate.
- Second, it should tax all income once and only once, without punishing or favoring one kind over another.
- Third, it should allow families to provide for themselves before they provide for the government.

Let's begin with the single rate. Aside from the fairness of treating everyone the same, it is the only way to keep a tax system simple. The moment we have more than one rate, the problem with enforcement rises exponentially.

The reason our current code requires such a vast and intrusive bureaucracy is that government must trace vast amounts of investment income as it is paid to business owners. For instance, Americans file *one billion* 1099 forms just to report investment income. With the single rate, all investment income can be taxed at the business end, rendering all those forms unnecessary.

Nobody has explained this better than the president's own head of the Council of Economic Advisors, Joseph Stiglitz, in his textbook *Economics of the Public Sector*: "The uniformity of [flat] marginal tax rates ... means that income can be taxed at its source; taxing income at its source will reduce compliance costs and increase compliance rates."

The next principle is that all income should be taxed once and only once—that is, the tax should be neutral. It should not discriminate against or favor certain kinds of

51

income. Here we get to the heart of what the flat tax is all about. As Alvin Rabushka puts it, the flat tax will remove the tax code from the economy. He means that while the tax code must collect the necessary amount of revenue to pay for government, it should not influence our decisions about how much to save and buy, what we should consume or how we should invest, how much we should work or what kind of work we should do.

That's what I mean by neutrality. A fair tax code is an impartial tax code. It is not for politicians or aspiring social engineers to decide how the rest of us should behave. People should make those decisions for themselves. *That's* what America is all about. *That's* the meaning of freedom. It's also the soundest approach to economics.

Something's wrong when government offers a tax break for certain kinds of investments on the grounds that those investments, in its opinion, are "good." Congressional committees, the Commerce Department, the Brookings Institution—with all the bright minds and advanced degrees we'll find at each of these places—do not collectively have the wisdom of millions of Americans left to make their own economic choices. Who is a better judge of which investments are good, faraway politicians and policy experts, or the guy with his money and his family's future on the line?

Why the personal allowance? One very simple reason: Our first responsibility is to take care of ourselves and our families. Only when we earn enough for that should we have to offer up our tithe to government.

Under my proposal, personal allowances are as follows. A single person gets an exemption of $11,350. A married couple gets an exemption of exactly double that amount, $22,700. And parents may claim a deduction of $5,300 for each child.

You'll notice that the flat tax ends the marriage penalty—one of the more perverse features of the current tax code. Married couples pay higher taxes because the exemptions for two married people are not twice the amount for a single person.

If you're married and have two children, you would have to earn $33,300 before you owed a single tax dollar. A family of four earning $33,300 will pay no federal income tax. A family earning $50,000 will effectively pay 6 percent. A family making $200,000 will effectively pay 14 percent.

Beyond that one allowance to every taxpayer in America, and the child deduction for parents, everybody pays 17 percent. That's as fair as you get.

This basic personal allowance strikes me, in actual practice, as a lot more progressive than our supposedly progressive code. It will cover a far larger portion of a middle-class person's income than of a rich person's. If you're making hundreds of thousands of dollars each year, the allowance may not mean much. But if you're pulling down thirty, forty, or fifty thousand dollars, it's going to make all the difference in the world.

Simplicity, neutrality, and the right to support yourself before paying a nickel to the government—those are the three basic principles of a flat tax. Anybody who tries to sell you a flat-tax plan without them isn't selling you a real flat tax.

What *is* open to discussion is the tax rate and the level of the exemptions. If you want the tax code more progressive, raise the family exemption. If, like me, you want the government to be smaller and collect less revenue, choose a low rate. If you favor a bigger government, go with the higher rate. As long as the structure of the plan remains—a single tax rate applied after family exemptions to all income—these points are debatable.

Why 17 Percent?

As a purely philosophical point, I happen to think even 17 percent is still too much. Offhand, it's about 7 percent too much.

In Dick Armey's America, the income tax would never rise above 10 percent.

My "model" for this belief, to borrow the jargon of economists, is the biblical tithe. I've always thought that if 10 percent is sufficient for God, it ought to be sufficient for government. I know it won't seem a compelling argument to fellow economists, but, well, it's a good enough model for me.

I set the rate at 17 percent because I wanted to provide a substantial tax cut. The Beltway types often talk as if any tax reform must be "revenue neutral"—that it brings in the same amount as the current tax system. I reject that. I refuse to be locked in by the spending levels of forty years of big government liberalism.

Come to think of it, the only time I ever hear them insisting on revenue neutrality is when we're trying to cut taxes and cut spending. It doesn't seem to work the other way: When they try to raise taxes and increase spending, revenue neutrality is never the benchmark.

Deficit neutrality is an entirely different matter. I certainly would not support any plan that will prevent us from reaching a balanced budget by the year 2002—a cardinal aim of the new Republican Congress.

By even the most conservative estimates of future economic growth, a 17-percent rate—with relatively modest spending cuts—will allow us to cut taxes, reform the tax system, but still achieve a balanced budget by 2002.

What It Means to You

Now let's take a deeper look at how the flat tax would work, keeping in mind that all you have to do is apply the three principles I listed above.

What about estate taxes?

Under the flat tax, there would be no estate taxes. Why? Because all income will be taxed once and only once. The flat-tax system recognizes that this money was earned and saved by someone else, and taxed along the way. For the state to come back and tax it *again*, merely because the earner has passed on and left it to you, is a form of double taxation and a violation of the second principle. It's an act of governmental grave robbing that also discourages people from saving, so as not to leave their heirs with the current 55-percent estate tax. Under the flat tax—no estate taxes, period.

What about investment income?

Exactly the same principle, applying to all investment income large and small.

"As a retired person with minimal income from investments resulting in little or no taxes," writes a flat-tax supporter in Cincinnati, "I'm still required to file from 60 to 110 pages over the past ten years with each 1040 form. For this I pay an accountant many hundreds of dollars each year because the tax code is beyond my comprehension."

There are all sorts of reasons this man should not have to be bothered with all those forms. But the biggest reason of all is that his dividends, however small, have *already* been taxed.

Under today's code, virtually all investment income is taxed at least twice: Once at the source—the business receiving the income; and again when it reaches the investor as personal income. (And if he were to leave those small stocks and dividends to an heir, it would be taxed a third time.) Under the flat tax, all investment income will be taxed once, only once, and at the source.

What's true of this taypayer and his humble dividends will be just as true of the big-time investor raking in millions: Every dollar he or she makes in investment income will be taxed at 17 percent before it even reaches him or her, but not again.

Inevitably, the class warriors will say that under a flat

55

tax the rich aren't being taxed on their interest income. One could explain it a hundred different ways, and still they'd insist that investment income was escaping taxes.

I don't see why it's so hard to understand. In my whole working life, I don't think I've ever sent a check off to the IRS. Does that mean I haven't been paying taxes all these years? No. By the time I get each paycheck, my employer has already removed my taxes and sent the money to the IRS. In the same way, under the flat tax, businesses pay taxes on the earnings business owners accumulate and send them to the IRS. A dividend or interest check is an after-tax payment, just like a paycheck.

To understand the current system of double taxation on investment income, imagine you got your paycheck, with taxes withheld—and then had to pay another tax on what was left!

What about savings and pensions?

Again the rule to remember is this: Under the flat tax, all income will be taxed once—but only once.

Under the current system, you pay taxes when you earn income, and then pay additional taxes when it is saved. A flat tax wouldn't tax you again if you decided to save it.

Here's how it would work. Because employers can deduct pension contributions, people would pay taxes on pension benefits when they received them. That's one tax. Income that we save outside of employer-sponsored savings plans would get the same treatment. When you earn a dollar of income, you pay the tax. But you don't pay taxes in the future.

Under a flat tax, we either tax what you put into savings and not tax it again when it comes out, or allow a deduction for what employers put in but tax it when it comes out. The flat tax catches all that income either coming or going. The current system catches savings coming *and* going.

What about Social Security?

Under the flat tax, Social Security benefits would not be taxed. The money you put into Social Security will already have been taxed.

What It Means to Businesses

The purpose of the business tax is not to tax businesses. Businesses don't pay taxes—people do. The purpose of the business tax is to tax business *income*. That means the income you make renting out the extra bedroom in your house, the income from a law partnership, or the income of General Motors.

Here's the flat-tax business tax form (which, along with the individual tax form, is one of the only two forms in the entire flat-tax system):

Form 2 ARMEY-SHELBY FLAT TAX FORM 1998	
Business Name	Employer Id Number
Street address	County
City, State and ZIP code	Principal Product

1 Gross revenue from sales	
2 Allowable costs	
(a) Purchases of goods, services, and materials	— — — — —
(b) Wages, salaries, and pensions	— — — — —
(c) Purchases of capital equipment, structures, and land	— — — — —
3 Total allowable costs [sum of lines 2(a), 2(b), 2(c)]	
4 Taxable income (line 1 less line 3)	
5 Tax (17% of line 4)	
6 Carry-forward from 1997	
7 Interest on carry-forward (6% of line 6)	
8 Carry-forward into 1988 (line 6 plus line 7)	
9 Tax due (line 5 less line 8, if positive)	
10 Carry-forward to 1999 (line 8 less line 5, if positive)	

It will be quite common in the flat-tax world for individuals to send in both forms. A farmer, for example, or a sole proprietor would file both forms, one covering any income he may receive from a salary, the other covering the income from his business activities.

Under the flat tax, businesses will pay 17 percent on total revenues minus expenses. Business revenue means all forms of income that are not taxed at the individual level. This includes corporate, sole proprietorship, and partnership income; interest income, rental profits, royalties, farming income—you name it.

What expenses are deductible? If you look at the form, you'll see that businesses can deduct wages and pension contributions. This is because individuals already report that income and pay tax on it.

You'll also notice that businesses can deduct the purchases they make from other businesses that are a cost of doing business. This includes the full cost of plant, equipment, and land.

This is a *huge* change from the current system. Right now, businesses can deduct the cost of new equipment, but only over a number of years according to very complicated depreciation schedules. These schedules are arcane and arbitrary and there are hundreds of them.

The flat tax would replace all of them by allowing an immediate deduction: The entire cost of new equipment may be written off in the same year the investment is made. Expensing, as this practice is called, is far more fair to the business. Under depreciation schedules, today's business owner often discovers that by the time he's through writing off a new machine, inflation has eroded the value of the deduction and he has, in effect, been paying extra taxes on investments made long ago. If he's allowed to deduct it all today, though, this hidden tax cannot be imposed.

Moreover, the depreciation schedules add enormous complexity to the tax system. If a company buys some new computers and can only deduct the expense gradually, according to some asset-value scheme dreamed up by a government bureaucrat, it faces a paperwork nightmare. That's a waste of time and resources.

And, of course, both of these consequences of today's depreciation schedule can mean only one thing: Businesses are investing far less than they should in order to evade the burdens of complying with the current tax code.

The flat tax would fix that. Again, the principles are that all income in the economy is taxed once and only once, and in the simplest way possible. If any expense is going to be or has been taxed elsewhere, it's deductible. If not, it's taxable.

After expenses are deducted, everybody from the corner grocer to the Fortune 500 company pays 17 percent. If net earnings are $50,000, the company pays a tax of $8,500. If net earnings are $100,000, the company owes $17,000. If net earnings are a billion dollars—$170 million.

For class warriors who fear the corporate big shots are going to make a killing under the flat tax, let me just say that by my reckoning $170 million—or a comparable amount—still comes to a pretty stout tax bill.

The difference, under a flat tax, is that every company in America will actually be *paying* their full tax bill. No more tax breaks or any of the other nonsense most of us rightly think of as "corporate welfare." No more intricate tax maneuvering; no more scurrying for shelter: Just pay your 17 percent and get on with the business, as most entrepreneurs would prefer to do anyway.

In the next chapter I'll try to convey those overall effects in more detail. Theory, practice, and common sense alike all tell us that under a flat tax our whole economy will thrive. Less time will be wasted on tax compliance, more time spent working and thinking and creating—above all creating jobs. Taxes will be lower, the incentives to tax avoidance fewer, yielding more revenue for the legitimate purposes of government.

Chapter 7

The Coming Flat-Tax Boom

"This law, if enacted, would free up millions of dollars for investment in the economy and bring about unprecedented economic prosperity," says a supporter from Cerritos, California.

I don't know if this letter writer has any formal economic training, but his common-sense understanding of flat-tax economics is shared by the nation's leading economists. They look into the future and see a coming flat-tax boom.

Dale Jorgenson, chairman of the economics department at Harvard University, concludes that if the flat tax had been enacted back in 1986 (the last time we tried major tax reform), our national wealth today would be one trillion dollars greater than it is now. Put another way, had we gone with the flat tax ten years ago, every American would now be $4,000 richer.

Jorgenson says that if we adopt the flat tax today, the economy will be 15 to 20 percent larger within a decade than it would otherwise be. That means trillions of dollars in additional national income. Under the flat tax, the typical family will see its annual income rise by $5,000 to $7,000 in only five years.

The authors of the plan, Robert Hall and Alvin Rabushka, surveyed the academic tax literature and used only the most conservative studies to produce a bare minimum estimate of the flat tax's benefits. If we enact the flat tax today, they concluded, by the year 2002, Americans will see a 6 percent rise in income—about $1,900 additional income for every man, woman, and child in America.

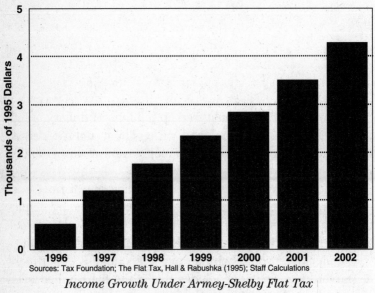

Sources: Tax Foundation; The Flat Tax, Hall & Rabushka (1995); Staff Calculations

Income Growth Under Armey-Shelby Flat Tax
(Family of Four at Median Income)

What these statistics portend is nothing less than a new era of unprecedented prosperity for America.

Why the Flat Tax Works

How will this happen? Very simple. The flat tax will sweep away nearly every one of the destructive features of our current tax code and let the American people do the rest.

• The end of high and rising marginal tax rates. After the personal allowance, all income will be taxed at 17 percent. More hard work won't mean higher tax brackets.

• Compliance costs will almost disappear. By one estimate, paying our taxes will cost America about 94 percent less than what it costs today.

• Income will be taxed only once; no more double taxing of savings and investments. Most investment income does not go to the bank accounts of millionaires, but to the pension and retirement programs of working and retired Americans. Thus people in all income groups will keep more of their own earnings.

• "Resources will find their most productive use," as the economic rule puts it. No more investments designed only to avoid or postpone the tax bill.

• More money will stay in the hands of the earner, instead of being siphoned off into wasteful government programs.

The net effect of a flat tax will be to restore the incentive to work, earn, save, and invest throughout our economy. It brushes aside all the low-growth dogmas of big government and takes us back to the simple wisdom of President Kennedy, who understood the relation between taxes and productivity:

"In short," he said in 1962, "it is a paradoxical truth that the tax rates are too high today and tax revenues are too low; and the soundest way to raise revenues in the long run is to cut taxes now. The purpose of cutting taxes now is not to incur a budget deficit, but to achieve the more prosperous, expanding economy which can bring a budget surplus."

Staggering Possibilities

A quick look at recent history—at least those brief periods when we followed a wise tax policy—provides a tantalizing hint of the spectacular economic growth we will enjoy under the flat tax.

In the same year John Kennedy spoke those words quoted above, he cut income taxes across the board. Around that time my job in life was to lay electric poles along a stretch of road in Cando, North Dakota, but I can still remember the spirit of the time, the opportunities that seemed to open up, the jolt those tax cuts gave our entire economy.

Under the tax cuts initiated by JFK, the top rate dropped from 91 percent to 70 percent. Still an incredibly high rate, but the cut was enough to get the American economy moving again, to move money away from tax shelters and foreign banks and back into productive enterprises.

Evidence of this could be seen in federal tax revenues. From 1963 to 1966, tax revenues actually rose by 16 percent. Tax collections from those earning $50,000 or more a year rose by 57 percent.

Most everybody, in other words, paid more in taxes because the whole economy was more active and most everybody was earning more. That's the paradox of supply-side economics, which is really not a paradox at all but common sense. When taxes are lower, there's more money available for investment and savings. When there's more investment, more things are produced and created. When that happens, wages go up and the general standard of living rises. The by-product of it all is higher tax revenue.

Exactly the same thing happened when President Reagan lowered the tax rates still further—to 28 percent. Again tax revenue went up dramatically. The share of income taxes paid by the top 10 percent of earners went from 48 percent to 57 percent in 1988. The richest 1 percent of Americans saw their share of total income taxes rise from 18 percent in 1981 to 28 percent in 1988.

Nobody but the usual class warriors complained because, while tax revenue was increasing, so was the income of most Americans. After the Reagan tax cuts:

- The entire economy grew by 31 percent in real terms (that is, allowing for inflation).
- Even as America's population rose by 28 million in the 1980s, the Gross National Product rose by 18 percent per person.
- The average income rose, in real terms, from $34,390 to $38,710—meaning that the typical family had 13 percent more money to spend or invest.
- The American people created over four million new businesses and 18.6 million new jobs, increasing total employment by 20 percent.
- Interest rates fell. New-home mortgage rates fell from 14.7 percent in 1982 to 8.07 percent in 1992. The prime rate fell from a high of 21.5 percent in 1981 to 6.5 percent in 1992.
- Manufacturing productivity grew by 3.4 percent per year.
- Our products became more competitive in markets abroad: The goods we shipped abroad nearly doubled, going from $213 billion in 1985 to $394 billion by the decade's end.

Mind you, even during these boom years, many of the problems in our tax code were almost as bad as they are today.

The rules were multiplying and getting more complex. Compliance costs were draining the economy of hundreds of billions of dollars.

Savings and investments were still being double taxed— giving us one of the lowest savings rates in the industrialized world.

Businesses and the self-employed were still contending with depreciation schedules and the like, instead of just deducting productive expenses outright.

The heirs to savings and small businesses were still paying unbearable estate taxes, forcing them to sell or close down thousands of family farms and shops.

Ronald Reagan accomplished many things, yet the tax code survived him. But think what that means: In the 1980s, we lowered the top rate to 28 percent, kept the double tax in place, tolerated our complex and costly tax code—and still got higher net incomes and higher tax revenues all at once.

The flat tax will lower the top rate to 17 percent, eliminate the double tax on investment, cut government spending, end estate taxes, and in one decisive blow render the tax code an historic relic. The possibilities are just staggering.

Rewarding an Honest Day's Work

These arguments from economic theory and practice are important, but in the end my own faith in the flat tax rests on the people of America who don't write studies or publish economic forecasts—the people who will actually make the investments and build the businesses.

The flat tax, as I've often said, bets on the goodness and sound judgment of the American people, not the guile of the federal government. It assumes that earnings are best left with the people, that they will spend their own money more wisely and more productively than even the most well intentioned government in the world. When they are left to make decisions, the economy will grow. When government tries to do it for them, the economy will suffer.

"As a businessman," writes a supporter from Los Angeles, "I can guarantee that the economy would take off like a rocket with this kind of tax structure, and the government would have more revenue than even they would know what to do with."

"For perhaps the first time in twenty-seven years," adds a woman from Patten, Maine, "I actually am excited about something as esoteric (to me) as tax reform legislation. Nothing against you or your colleagues, but I would just as soon spend or save as much as I could of the money I earn, rather than having it done for me."

"Keep up the pressure on the flat-tax issue," urges a man from Houston. "You will see a massive surge in the economic activity with a flat, predictable, known, nonretroactive tax structure. First, all the bright lawyers and accountants can go to work on wealth-creating projects instead of feeding on it."

"It seems so obvious out here," writes a supporter from Mercer Island, Washington, "that the Republican Party could sweep both houses and the presidency if your proposals were the principal plank of the party and each candidate made it the central issue of their campaign. The beneficiaries of big government, mostly the bureaucrats, will fight you to the end, but the great middle class . . . the ones left in private industry, the small business operator for example, will vote in droves given the chance and a real choice."

Much as I agree with the last letter writer's electoral analysis, the flat tax is not a partisan issue. It will succeed not because of any one party's domination in Washington, and not because one economic class will assert itself over another. Ultimately, I believe the flat tax will move the whole tax debate beyond the shallow class-war rhetoric that used to divide us.

All Americans—rich, poor, or like most of us in-between—share the same basic interests in a growing economy and a fair, impartial tax system. Driving the flat-tax cause movement is not greed; just about the farthest thing from it: the simple desire to care for our families, to make our way in the world as free men and women, and to claim the rewards of an honest day's work.

Chapter 8

"I'm for a Flat Tax, But . . ."

The best homage to the power of the flat-tax idea is that many in Washington are today rushing forward with flat-tax plans of their own. Everybody wants in, even people who just a few years ago seemed quite content with our current tax code. The scene reminds me of George C. Scott as "The Flim-Flam Man" advising his younger partner on how to handle trouble: "Son, when you're bein' run outta town, just get out in front and make it look like a parade."

But when you hear people saying "I'm for a flat tax," listen carefully. All but two candidates for the presidential nomination have come out for some sort of flat tax. Their refrain has been: "I'm for a flat tax, but I want to keep the (fill in the blank) deduction." Usually it's the mortgage and/or charitable deductions. Keeping any deductions—especially the mortgage deduction—seriously changes the nature of the flat tax. I'll deal with this a little later.

I've looked over all these alternative plans, which are offered with varying degrees of seriousness. As near as I can tell they amount to the ringing statement, "I'm for a flat tax, but let's keep the current system, too!" First, though, let's dispense with the Democratic version of "I'm for a flat tax, but . . ."

Take, for example, the plan offered up recently by the leading House Democrat. So far the details have yet to be hammered out. There isn't even a bill before the House. The plan consists of a press release sent out to the media a few months ago, heralded on the news that night as the "Democratic alternative" to my flat-tax bill, and then apparently filed away and forgotten.

Assuming, though, the actual bill will one day materialize, let me describe it. Under the sponsor's visionary scheme, we would scrap our current five-rate income tax and replace it with . . . five *new* rates. I call it visionary because the sponsor is the only one I know of who can look at those five rates—ranging from 10 percent to 34 percent—and see a flat-tax rate.

He assures us, however, that even with those five rates, we would still enjoy all the benefits of simplicity. We'd even get the postcard. The difference is, his postcard-sized tax form is merely the cover page to a sheaf of forms and instructions and schedules not much thinner than today's bundle from the IRS.

For example, we would still need to file a Schedule B for interest and dividend income and a Schedule D for capital gains income. Then there's the Schedule A, C, and E. And let's not forget Schedules F, R, and SE. At the same time, millions of elderly Americans would still have to calculate the amount of Social Security income subject to tax. As for the majority of Americans who today are able to file without itemizing, under the plan in the press release they would henceforth be required to include health benefits as part of their income. Take out your calculators!

For those with pension income, the press-release plan offers a challenging new set of calculations to estimate the inside buildup of the pension.

And finally, on the business side, three of the most complex areas of the code appear unchanged at all: depreciation schedules, the treatment of foreign source income, and pension rules.

So much for scrapping the tax code. A nice try, but this is not what most of us have in mind when we think tax reform.

In fact, until recently, it was not what many prominent Democrats themselves had in mind. Listen, for example, to my old House colleague Leon Panetta, now White House Chief of Staff. Much as I'd like to claim credit for being a legislative pioneer for the flat tax, Leon, in fact, beat me to it by a good ten years:

> I believe what the country needs—and what the American people want—is a return to a fair and simple system of taxation. The legislation I am introducing today would . . . eliminate virtually all deductions, credits, and exclusions. . . . The system encourages taxpayers to direct their resources toward investments which have no economic or productive value other than reducing their tax burden.

As if that weren't a thorough enough indictment of the tax code, Representative Panetta went on to explain the deeper problem:

> The primary reason for this increasing complexity is the continuing use of the code as a vehicle for achieving societal goals that are unrelated to the raising of revenue. While we may agree with many of these goals, the laws tangled together are a tangled mess, making it extremely difficult for

most taxpayers to understand their rights and
responsibilities.

I leave it for Panetta to explain what caused him to lose
his tax reform zeal. In any case, his critique *then* is no less
true *today.* The code hasn't gotten any simpler.

Equally curious is the change of position I've noticed
over at *The Washington Post.* Most of us, when we read what
The Washington Post or some other newspaper has to say on
some weighty question or other, attach significance to it. It's
an institution addressing us, reflecting the collective wisdom
of the paper's senior scribes. Either that, or, as the paper's
treatment of the flat-tax issue suggests, the *Post* is just some
guy sitting in a newsroom cubicle with his own opinions.

Here was the *Post* back in 1982, around the time of
Panetta's bill:

> The ideal income tax would be a flat percent-
> age of all income above an arbitrary threshold. . . .
> It would be simple, quick, and easy. . . . It would be
> no less fair than the present tangle . . . that [is] cur-
> rently producing . . . widespread public cynicism
> and hostility. A flat tax is the obvious remedy.

Flash forward to 1996. Here's the *Post*'s latest wisdom on
the flat tax:

> A flawed idea, less a serious tax proposal than
> a slogan in the name of which the advocates claim
> to be able to accomplish several contradictory
> things at once.

A similar conversion took place at *The New York Times,*
but in less time. This is the gray lady speaking in 1982:

Who can respect an income tax system that allows many wealthy citizens to pay little or no tax yet claims close to half the marginal earnings of the middle class? ... The most dramatic fresh start, without changing the total amount collected, would be a flat-rate tax levied on a greatly broadened income tax base.

When Jerry Brown came along with his flat-tax plan in the 1992 primary campaign, the *Times* immediately saw serious flaws: It wasn't flat enough. It wasn't—well, best to let the *Times* make the point for me:

Tax reform should also simplify the code, making loopholes harder for Congress to disguise, and enact. And for reasons of elementary decency, tax reform shouldn't come at the expense of the poor.

Such was the paper's zeal for the idea that it even lionized Hall and Rabushka, praising the two for their "superb idea." I hope they kept that clip for their scrapbook, because now, judging by recent *Times* editorials, it turns out the whole thing isn't such a hot idea after all.

"Flat taxes," said the *Times* in January 1996, "have a glaring fault. They lower tax burdens on the richest families and raise them on many working-class families." Longtime readers should forget all that stuff about the importance of investment capital—"what the economy needs to grow." It turns out the integration of business and individual taxes "would shift taxes away from wealthy shareholders."

So much for institutional consistency. Both papers, of course, are entitled to change policy on such issues. Like most Americans, I suspect, I was influenced by them one way or the other. Let's remember these examples when we hear politicians promising to support a flat tax. Make sure they mean it. On the stump and in the editorial pages, sometimes all the big talk can be translated as a resounding: "I'm for a flat tax, but don't hold me to it."

Chapter 9

Stay Flat or Die

"I'm for a flat tax, but I want to keep the mortgage and charitable deductions."

This is roughly the position of all the leading GOP candidates but one. Understandably, they are wary of offending voters who lean to the flat tax but fear losing their deductions, especially the home mortgage interest deduction. I sympathize with the candidates' reluctance to take on the tax code pure and simple and put an end to all deductions: It's not the easiest thing to explain when you're out on the stump running for president.

Announce that you're going to end deductions, and within thirty-six hours you can switch on the local TV station and see the inevitable attack ad: "Senator X says he's going to *take away your mortgage deduction! Don't let him do it! Vote for me and I'll save you!*" Accompanying the charges will be images of middle-class families being evicted from their homes into snowy streets, or mean-looking bankers in starchy suits stamping FORECLOSURE on a deed of trust.

I understand all the pragmatic considerations facing candidates who might otherwise endorse a flat tax, period. I just happen to think it underestimates the power of the flat-tax movement and intelligence of most taxpayers.

The Mortgage Deduction

"I personally have what I consider to be a large mortgage on my home," says a recent letter from Lessburg, Florida, "but I'm willing to give this up for a flat tax."

I hear that a lot. I wouldn't go so far as to say it's a resounding majority: Of course the voters are concerned about the loss of deductions. I would be, too. But that doesn't mean Republicans should run for cover, and it certainly doesn't give us license to exploit the issue with the cheap class war rhetoric of the left. It just means the voters want an explanation. Let's give it a try right here.

At the moment the charges we hear leveled against the flat tax can be summarized as follows:

• Without their mortgage deduction, millions of home owners would be unable to pay the interest on home loans.

• Loss of the mortgage deduction would wreck home values, eroding or erasing owners' equity.

• The entire housing industry would suffer as foreclosure rates doubled and, without the deduction, millions more Americans would find themselves unable to afford a house.

Each of these would be true *if* the elimination of the mortgage deduction occurred in a vacuum. But it won't: What we're talking about here is a complete scrapping of the tax code. The whole point of the flat tax is to leave taxpayers with a lot more of their own money in the first place. Under a flat tax, home owners won't need deductions any more than businesses will need tax breaks.

The mortgage deduction is the classic example of government offering help with problems largely of its own making. Why, under the current tax code, do we even need the mortgage deduction?

• The average family today is paying anywhere from 30 to 40 percent of its income to government—15 to 25 percent in federal taxes.

• Interest rates are so high—in large part because interest income is taxable under today's code.

• Excessive regulation by the federal government has today added an average of $4,000 to the price of a house.

Under the flat tax, the first two problems will not exist anymore. The third will begin to pass away as the housing industry becomes less taxed and regulated.

Interest income will no longer be taxable: Borrowers won't deduct interest paid, but lenders won't pay tax on interest received. Lenders will accept lower rates, and thus the interest rate will drop. In other words, home owners will gain in lower rates what they lose in the mortgage interest deduction.

What's more, if savings rates rise, as they would under the flat tax, the decline in interest rates would be even greater.

The following table shows the amount the typical family deducts for mortgage interest and the amount the deduction reduces its tax liability. It also shows much the same family would save in lower interest payments if the interest rate dropped by 25 percent—the drop projected by John Golob, an economist with the Federal Reserve.

Income	$20,000	50,000	75,000	100,000	200,000
Average Mortgage Deduction[1]	1,067	3,834	7,693	10,410	18,051
Taxes Saved from Deduction	160	575	2,154	2,915	5,596
Savings from Lower Interest Rate[2]	267	959	1,923	2,603	4,513
Gain from Flat Tax[3]	107	384	(231)	(312)	(1,083)

Interest Deduction Versus Lower Interest Rates

1. Source: Price Waterhouse.

2. Assumes an interest rate drop of 25 percent, based on a study by Federal Reserve economist John Golob. See "How Would Tax Reform Affect Financial Markets?" *Economic Review*, Federal Reserve Bank of Kansas City, Fourth Quarter 1995.

3. This gain only looks at the interest costs in isolation. It does not include the benefit of the lower tax rate, the high family exemption, higher economic growth, and lower compliance costs.

For Americans who pay a 15 percent marginal rate, which is most taxpayers, a 25 percent drop in interest rates makes them better off—even if the home mortgage deduction is eliminated.

For a family earning $50,000 and deducting $3,834 in mortgage interest, the lower interest rates save it $959—or $384 more than the home mortgage deduction saves it under the current code.

For a family earning $100,000 and deducting $10,410 in home mortgage interest, switching to a flat tax would more or less be a wash. Rather than deducting $2,915 in interest payments, the lower tax rates would reduce the payment by $2,602, a difference of $312.

These figures do not include other benefits of a flat tax, such as lower compliance costs and higher economic growth. Moreover, while fewer than half of home owners claim the mortgage deduction, *all* Americans would stand to gain from lower interest rates.

Note, too, the progressive element in all this: Right now the value of the mortgage interest deduction is greatest for those with the largest incomes. If you're paying a mortgage on a million-dollar house, you're claiming a deduction worth five times that of the person paying interest on a $200,000 house. In fact, 88 percent of those who do deduct have incomes above $50,000.

The mortgage deduction is more the rich man's issue than a middle-class issue. Middle-class home owners have more to gain under a flat tax, because the value of their increased after-tax income is that much greater percentage-wise.

The polls, incidentally, bear this out. In a survey taken in July of last year, recent home buyers were asked what they thought most important in deciding whether to buy a house. The graph shows the results:

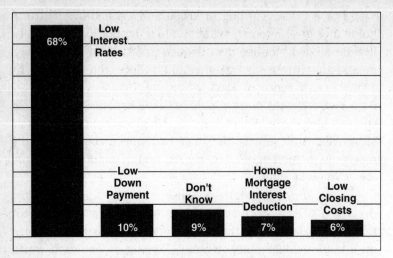

*Which is most important to you in making
the purchase of a home affordable?*

By an almost ten-to-one margin home buyers put interest
rates above the deduction. By decisive majority, respondents
said they were willing to give up the home mortgage deduction if their taxes were reduced by an equal amount—as will
happen under the flat tax.

When you hear about studies finding that the flat tax will
hurt home owners, always consider the source. If the study
was paid for by a special interest Washington lobby, you
should beware.

Take one example, for instance. Many claims that the
flat tax will depress home values come from one flawed study
by DRI/McGraw Hill, an economic consulting firm-for-hire.
The study was financed with $70,000 from—surprise—the Na-
tional Association of Realtors.

Predictably, it reaches conclusions suitably hysterical for
its $70,000 price tag, finding that the flat tax will lower hous-
ing values by 15 percent. When the study was exposed to
legitimate scrutiny, though, it fell apart. It turns out DRI

analyzed a completely hypothetical flat-tax plan with a rate of
25 percent, fully five percentage points above by initial rate of
20 percent and eight points over my fully phased-in rate of 17
percent. But no one was proposing a plan with a rate of 25
percent. That subtlety, of course, was lost in many of the
scary news accounts generated by the report.

Hired-gun special interest consulting firms are familiar
to tax reformers. Birnbaum and Murray tell a story in *Gucci
Gulch* of real estate lobbyists trying to save deductions for va-
cation homes in the 1986 tax reform bill:

> To help make his argument, Franks [a real es-
> tate lobbyist] called in Jesse Abraham, an econo-
> mist . . . to conduct a study on the economic effects
> of the proposed second-home limitation. Such sup-
> posedly objective studies were a standard part of
> the Washington lobbyist's repertoire. "What do you
> think you'll find?" Franks asked. Abraham re-
> sponded, "First of all, I don't have a contract with
> you or a check from you." After Franks ordered up
> a check and a contract, Abraham inquired, "What
> do you want us to find?"

Who did this Abraham work for? DRI—the same firm
now attacking the flat tax with the best study money can buy.
I think you get the picture.

A recent study by the Heritage Foundation, a nonpartisan think tank committed to limited government, reached a
different conclusion. Here's what Heritage's economists
found: "The historical relationship between personal income
growth and the value of owner-occupied housing, combined
with the range of estimates showing faster economic growth
under a flat tax—shows that home values actually will rise by
as much as 7 to 14 percent by the fifth year after enactment
of the flat tax." That's a 7 percent increase *minimum*.

The NAR example is a perfect case of what I call Institutional Potomac Fever. The Washington office of the NAR isn't representing the nation's Realtors, but instead looking out for the interests of the Washington lobbyists. A recent poll of registered Realtors conducted by the Polling Company on January 26–29, 1996, shows they think the tax code should be reformed and, by a two-to-one margin, would be willing to give up their own home mortgage interest deduction if their tax bill wouldn't go up. But if there are no deductions, what reason will there be for the nation's Realtors to have a big staff and an expensive office in downtown Washington, D.C.?

The Charitable Deduction

A few years ago a fellow I know, then in his mid-twenties and newly married, got involved in a program sponsored by his church in Virginia to help pay the expense of kids in need of medical attention. A little boy in need of an eye operation was brought up from the island of St. Lucia and stayed with the couple for several months. They housed, fed, clothed, and looked after him the whole time. After the operation (unsuccessful, as it turned out) the boy went back home.

Not once in this whole time did the man ever pause to consider the tax advantage of all this. Only later did it even occur to him that these expenses could be deducted, and by then, he figured, it was too late.

It's a nice thing that such people today can, if they choose, write off the costs of their good deeds. But in fact my friend's case is fairly typical: A good portion of total charitable giving in America goes to churches and church-related charities. And very little of that amount is ever even deducted. Most people give for no other reason than to give.

Sure, sometimes the extra incentive of a deduction doesn't hurt. But to most Americans, a worthy cause is a worthy cause, and the statistics do not suggest that if the deduction were eliminated we would see a sudden cutoff in contributions to charitable causes.

Just the opposite: Even with the deduction, about half of all charitable contributions today are not even written off. In 1991, charitable causes around America received some $117 billion—yet only $61 billion was written off on personal tax returns.

The same thing could be seen during the 1980s. Under President Reagan, the top marginal rate was lowered to 50, then 28 percent. The charitable deduction thus became less valuable in proportion to taxes paid. If charitable giving were determined by tax incentive alone, one might therefore expect giving to decline. The opposite happened—it actually *doubled*. Religious giving nearly *tripled*.

People do not need prodding from the federal government to give to charity. We know that helping others is a good thing—and we know it from a somewhat higher authority than the tax code.

Americans need such instruction least of all: Long before the welfare state, Americans were an example to the world in creating and financing private charities of every kind. And most were a lot more successful than the modern government in alleviating the social ills that concerned them.

As for the museums and opera companies and universities that today benefit from the charitable deduction, I'm sure they'll fare just fine in a flat-tax environment. The patrons of these institutions tend to be on the wealthy end anyway, and along with everyone else they, too, stand to gain from the overall economic benefits of a flat tax.

I have never understood why the taxpayers should in effect be subsidizing these things anyway—worthy as they are. No doubt I'll be called a philistine or worse for saying this, but their insistence on public support for such projects calls to mind one of Armey's Axioms: "It is always the most privileged who complain the loudest."

In any case, the best thing government can do to help charities of every kind is to leave individuals with more of their own earnings. Take a look at the chart below. It traces America's total personal income and total personal giving.

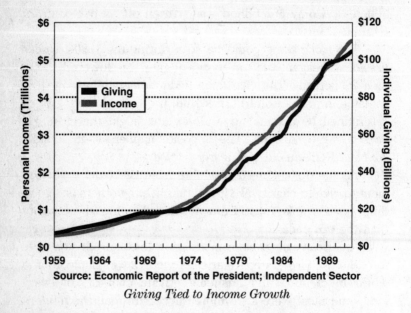

Source: Economic Report of the President; Independent Sector

Giving Tied to Income Growth

Nothing too complex there: The more money we have to call our own, the more money we give to others.

A final point—and it goes back to what I said in the introduction about the very idea of deductions.

By definition, a deduction is something granted by government. It can let you keep a deduction. It can reduce your deduction. Or, as invariably happens, it can just let your deduction erode away over the years by inflation.

Forty years ago, for example, the personal deduction was $600. In inflation-adjusted dollars, that would come to something like $6,000 today instead of the $2,450 the government now grants us.

The flat tax presents home owners, and every other taxpayer in America, with this question: Would you rather live your life dependent upon the whims of government, or would you rather keep more of your own money and manage your own affairs?

I admit there's a certain security in sticking with things as they are, clinging to our deductions and breaks. At least we know the system. But that attitude reminds me of a news article I once read about a guy who petitioned a judge for permission to remain in prison even though his sentence had ended. Apparently he'd grown so used to life there that he couldn't bear to leave it. He knew everybody, knew what to expect each day, liked the security of his job in the laundry room. He just couldn't imagine anything else.

Many years of big government have had a similar effect on the American taxpayer. We may not like our tax situation, but we've become prisoners of the tax code, and with our little deductions and breaks there's something secure about it. In some ways we've forgotten how a free economy operates, a country where people aren't paying a king's ransom to government in the first place. Under the flat tax, we'll regain that freedom, and with it the much greater security freedom offers.

Chapter 10

Torturing the Data

"There are two distinct classes of men in the Nation," wrote Thomas Paine, "those who pay taxes and those who receive and live upon taxes. . . . When taxation is carried to excess it cannot fail to disunite the two."

This would be a rather elegant way of describing today's struggle for power between modern Washington and the taxpayers of America. But the same lines of force are at work, lines roughly corresponding to the Beltway that circles our capital. On the one side are those who benefit from big government and high taxes. On the other are those who pay the bills. In the flat-tax movement, we're seeing the inevitable revolt by the latter group against the former.

I don't want to be too scornful of those inside the Beltway whose livelihoods depend upon big government and high taxes. I'm sure many of them are acting by their own best lights: They truly believe the federal government should be involving itself in nearly every aspect of our daily lives, our private transactions, our important economic decisions. As they see it, this is a perfectly sound and principled way to run a country.

That's not how *I* read the Constitution; but, nevertheless,

DICK ARMEY

they're very sincere in their faith in big government. With equal sincerity they believe that the rest of us should be required to pay for it—whatever the cost.

That's one kind of person we find opposing the flat tax. Then there's the other kind Tom Paine was describing. They are the ones who live upon big government, enjoy the powers, privileges, and status it affords them, inhabit the Beltway culture, and regard any and all attempts to reform the tax code as a mortal threat.

This helps explain the desperation I've encountered among some critics of the flat tax. If they can't find enough to fault in the idea itself, the critics just make things up.

"Massive Budget Shortfall"

Let me give you an example of what I mean. One morning in the fall of 1994, I picked up my *Washington Post* to find a guest column by a fellow named Robert S. McIntyre attacking my Freedom and Fairness Restoration Act.

Why? Because, warned McIntyre, identified as director of something called Citizens for Tax Justice (CTJ), "Armey's bill would add massively to the federal budget deficit. In fact, a reasonable estimate—just confirmed by the Joint Committee on Taxation—is that Armey's proposal would cost the Treasury $200 billion a year."

The Joint Committee on Taxation is a nonpartisan office of Congress charged with economic analysis, and I didn't remember it ever making any such finding. I put the newspaper aside and called my economic adviser, Andrew Laperriere. "Andy, has the JCT estimated any deficit shortfall under my bill?"

The JCT had confirmed nothing of the sort. It hadn't even looked into the matter. The claim was pulled from thin air.

We got ahold of that study by CTJ. It ran all of one page,

but even in that short space it managed to contain an egregious error. For some inexplicable reason, they assumed that no tax would be paid on the $471 billion that people earn by selling goods and services to the federal government.

That is, when a private company sells a $1 billion warship—or whatever—to the government, the company is then taxed on that $1 billion. The shipyard workers, suppliers, and others are taxed in turn. The government collects those taxes. But the estimates used by CTJ take no account of such revenue.

My staff and I found that once that error was corrected, CTJ's numbers confirmed my own revenue estimates: a revenue loss of $22 billion under my plan.

When I first proposed my flat-tax bill, I estimated it would cause a $20 to $40 billion revenue loss in the first year. Unthinkable solution: *cut* federal spending, now at $1.5 trillion, by a comparable amount. In my bill I proposed just such cuts.

I had not heard the last from Citizens for Tax Justice. Their scholarship would show up again in another "study" produced for my friend Dick Gephardt, the House Minority Leader.

Relying on CTJ's work, Representative Gephardt charged that my plan would increase the tax bill of the typical American family of four by no less than $4,500. Worse yet, he says, it would also increase the federal deficit by $200 billion.

Already his critique begins to unravel: How could any plan raise the typical American's tax bill by thousands of dollars, and, at the same time, explode the deficit? The answer is: It can't.

Here's how Gephardt, with a little help from CTJ, cooked the books.

Step one: Rewrite my proposal. Where my flat tax provides for a family exemption of over $30,000, CTJ shrinks the family exemption to little more than $12,000—thus exposing

89

to tax thousands of dollars that would be exempt under my plan. The reason for reducing the exemptions, they say, is to make the proposal "revenue neutral."

Step two: Make a completely arbitrary determination about who pays business taxes. CTJ falsely assumes, among other things, that the incidence of today's corporate income tax falls exclusively on stockholders (rich folks), leaving the rest of us untouched. But the corporate income tax in Armey's bill—well, that's a different story. My corporate income tax, they assume, will hit the consumers of America, the middle class, everybody—sparing no one.

Even the Clinton Treasury Department restrained itself from making that claim. The fact is, the same people would pay either business tax.

So much for the alleged tax increase. How about the charge that the flat tax will bust the budget?

That brings us to:

The final step: Ignore previous steps. Recall that they slashed the family allowance in my bill to make it revenue neutral. If Gephardt rewrote my bill to make it revenue neutral, how could it now increase the deficit, too?

His own misrepresentations contradict each other.

Apparently, CTJ has a history of this sort of thing. They gave Jerry Brown's flat-tax proposal in 1992 the same treatment—preparing studies, issuing press releases, writing urgent op-eds denouncing the flat tax. Even Alexander Cockburn of the left-wing *Nation* dismissed CTJ's figures on the Brown plan as "tendentious to the point of outright dishonesty."

As for the claim of being a citizens' watchdog group, I've since learned a little more about CTJ itself. It turns out the outfit is bankrolled by organized labor. In fact it was founded in 1979 by the AFL-CIO to lobby for higher taxes on corporations. "The average taxpayer's voice in Washington" was how Dan Rostenkowski once lauded CTJ.

As of a few years ago, some 99 percent of CTJ's revenues—$266,000—was still coming from organized labor. On its thirty-two-member board are such champions of the American taxpayer as Lane Kirkland of the AFL-CIO, Owen Bieber of the UAW, and Joan Claybrook of Public Citizen—Ralph Nader's group.

As late as 1984, the very office space used by CTJ was lent by organized labor. The space was generously donated by the Service Employees International Union.

As for McIntyre himself, before becoming an expert on my flat-tax bill, he had been with Citizens for Tax Justice since 1980, prior to which he worked for Nader's now-defunct Tax Reform Research Group. His predecessor in that post was David C. Wilhelm, who went on to become chairman of the Democratic National Committee until relieved of his duties after the 1994 election.

The Leaking Treasury

A similar chain of events began just before the '94 election. This time the statistics in question came from the Treasury Department.

One Sunday afternoon about ten days before the election, my deputy chief of staff, Brian Gunderson, got a call from a reporter for *The Washington Post*. The reporter had just been leaked a Treasury study. It purported to show that the flat tax would increase the deficit by $246 billion annually. To cover the shortfall and remain "revenue neutral," it said, the flat rate would have to be 25.8 percent.

Of course it was leaked on a Sunday to leave my staff and me no time to see it before it hit the Monday papers. To my knowledge, Treasury has never before or since produced a study on a bill that was not being considered by committee in Congress. This was a first.

A few days later we would discover a *$500 billion* error.

The Treasury study arbitrarily assumed that my proposal would permit over $500 billion in deductions that it wouldn't. By adding these deductions, Treasury incorrectly reduced the tax base and came up with a false deficit prediction.

It wasn't long before Treasury officials admitted publicly that their study was wrong. A second study then estimated that a flat rate of 23 percent would be needed to make my proposal revenue neutral.

I'm afraid there were problems there, too. So Treasury produced a third study. Now the necessary rate fell to 20.8 percent. Down further. I'm still holding out for a fourth study, which at this rate may well show that a flat tax would pay off the national debt.

At a 17 percent rate, said the third study—the last to date—the flat-tax plan would cost the federal government $138 billion. In other words, we'd be left with a deficit that much bigger.

But that too was another case of torturing the statistics until they confessed to anything. For starters, Treasury simply disregarded the three-year transition provided for in Armey-Shelby. Under the bill, the flat income tax rate for all Americans would be 20 percent for the first two years. Then we'd move to the permanent rate of 17 percent. Without that transition, *and* the budget cut of $40 billion, of course there would be a major shortfall. That's why we included them.

Chapter 11

The National Sales Tax

What about a national sales tax? Some prominent tax-cutters, as gung-ho as I am for scrapping the current income tax code, have suggested that we replace it instead with a national sales tax. The idea is to place a 20- or 25-percent tax on nearly everything we buy.

It has some of the virtues of the flat tax. A sales tax could also have one rate, be fair to everyone, and benefit the economy. Even more, it would abolish the income tax entirely. Many of its boosters, in fact, plan to repeal the Sixteenth Amendment, taking away the government's authority to levy any income tax at all.

Of course, that's where the trouble starts. Repealing a constitutional amendment is as difficult as passing one, and there's no way in my considered judgment that the Sixteenth is ever going to be repealed. We'd need to get the votes of 290 members of the House, 67 members of the Senate, and a majority of the legislatures of three-quarters of the states. As I count the votes, that isn't going to happen.

It doesn't take a cynic to see what that means. If we try to move to a national sales tax and fail to take away the government's authority to levy an income tax, we're going to get

Dick Armey's worst nightmare and a big spender's paradise: both a national sales tax *and* an income tax.

But even if we could safely make the jump to a sales tax, it would still be a boon for the big spenders, for this reason: It's hidden.

With a national sales tax, your tax bill will be concealed in the price of nearly everything you buy. You'll take a product to the cash register, the clerk will quote you the price, and you'll lay your money down, hardly realizing the amount of the tax included.

Sure, if you check the receipt, you'll notice the tax bill, but how many of us will do that? Cast your mind back over the last few weeks and just try to estimate what you paid in sales taxes on everything you bought. Ask people leaving a store how much they paid only a moment earlier in sales taxes. No one will be able to tell you. Most of us pay no attention to the sales levy; we just automatically think of it as part of the prices we pay.

With a national sales tax in place, politicians will quickly discover that they can raise taxes with impunity.

Of course, they might have trouble collecting the money. One thing they will quickly find under any national sales tax is that it will lead to massive tax evasion. This is a little ironic since one of the purported virtues of the sales tax is that it will eliminate the underground economy. I don't quite follow the reasoning, but they seem to think that the same people who today dodge our complicated income tax system won't try to dodge the sales tax.

Just wait. If we had a national sales tax high enough to fund the government, there would need to be a 20- or 25-percent tax slapped on consumer goods. The price of almost everything would rise by one-quarter. *But people will not pay such a high tax.*

As the incentive to evade grows, under a sales tax the opportunities for evasion multiply: Businesses will find ways to label their consumer goods tax-exempt wholesale items. They will purchase goods in a cash black market. All sorts of possibilities for evasion would open up. A sales tax, in short, will be immediately undermined by a silent tax revolt.

The bureaucrats in Canada learned this lesson the hard way. Shortly after Ottawa imposed its goods and services tax, the Canadian numbers crunchers noticed that the tax was bringing in far less money than expected. Coincidentally, the Canadian treasury soon noticed a dramatic increase in what it called real currency flowing through the economy. Why were Canadians suddenly using so much cash? Guess.

Actually, nearly all the industrial countries that imposed a sales tax find that it doesn't work and they quickly try some extreme means to stop the massive evasion. They begin by trying to collect a new tax at the cash register, and soon they have no choice but to extend that tax beyond the retailer to every level of production, as they desperately try to stop inevitable and massive tax evasion. In 1967, twenty-one developed countries had retail, wholesale, manufacturer, or multistage sales taxes. Today, twenty out of twenty-one of these national sales taxes have become value added taxes. Every developed country except Australia that has had a sales tax now has a VAT. Don't think it won't happen here. "There is no surer art one government learns from another," as Adam Smith observed, "than the art of taking money from the pockets of the people."

By this point, you must be wondering what happened to our goal of simplicity. By simple, I mean not only quick and uncomplicated, but also minimal involvement by tax collector in the life of taxpayer. Under a flat income tax, we just send in a single form and don't hear from the IRS again until next time. Under a sales tax, paying federal taxes becomes a daily activity: Every retail store in America becomes a branch office of the IRS, and every business person becomes a tax collector. In effect the IRS would be contracting out to every business in America and hovering nearby as the invisible partner in every economic transaction. Taxpaying should be done in the privacy of one's own home.

It's true of course that businesses already collect taxes for the government. But there's one big difference: Today, businesses collect a relatively small share of taxes in America. Three-quarters of the income in our economy is labor income, paid by individuals. But under a national sales tax, there is no direct tax on individuals, so businesses would assume the full responsibility for tax collection. Every retailer in America would be moonlighting as an IRS agent—hardly the dream of America's entrepreneurs.

Even if we assume the best case—no VAT—there would still be problems. It would be an administrative mess. A national sales tax would probably exempt many basic necessities from tax—beginning with food and clothing. This would lead to disputes over real clothes versus accessories, or nutritional food versus snack food—with the federal government left to sort things out. I can just hear the arguments from the inevitable lobbyists representing Hostess cupcakes: "Look at the label—it's *bread*!"

Worse, the federal sales tax and the dozens of different state sales taxes—aside from having different rates—would likely exempt different taxes. That means a small-business owner would have to look up the correct state sales tax rate, apply the federal rate, subtract the state sales tax rate from items exempted by only the state, or subtract only the federal rate from items federal-only exempted. Then he would have to do separate calculations for each of the states in which he does business. And so on.

Finally, I doubt that under a sales tax most of us would even be freed from the trouble of filing. Even if the basic necessities of life were exempted—the sales tax's version of a personal exemption—many Americans would be unable to afford their full sales tax burden. This would mean rebates, with more paperwork and, of course, staggering possibilities for fraud. In every respect, a flat tax is a better alternative.

Chapter 12

The Flat Tax and the 1996 Election

If the folks inside the Beltway didn't notice the flat-tax bill back when I introduced it in 1994; they have by now. In the Republican primaries, just about every candidate has offered his own version of a flat-tax plan.

The early front-runner, Senator Bob Dole, campaigned on the promise of a "flatter-tax" system. This year he endorsed the findings of the Kemp Commission on Tax Reform—which recommends a single, flat tax rate. Pat Buchanan, for his part, is a longtime flat-taxer, at least in principle. While he was still in the race, Senator Phil Gramm offered his own version of a flat tax, keeping certain deductions while imposing a single income tax rate. Even those who opted not to run had been planning to campaign on a flat-tax platform, including former Vice President Quayle and Jack Kemp himself.

Early on, it was Steve Forbes who grabbed most of the attention. But well before his arrival, the campaign was shaping up as a contest of flat-tax proposals. That's how far the flat-tax cause has come in just two years—from the obscurity of academic journals, to the House floor, to near-unanimity among the Republican field of presidential candidates.

Talk about the power of an idea! Offhand, I cannot think of any idea that ever has advanced by such leaps and bounds in American politics.

When I laid my flat-tax bill on the clerk's desk in the House of Representatives in June of 1994, I felt it was a kind of Rubicon in American politics. What observers in Washington might regard as an eccentric and lonely gesture, I believed the American people would see much differently. In placing the bill before Congress, I felt that a new stage in the tax debate was about to begin. We would be calling the question, putting an end to years of pointless quarreling over the minutia of tax policy and taking on the code itself.

"Success," as the old adage goes, "is the child of audacity." In mid-1993, the cause of tax reform was in need of a little audacity. I believed only the boldest strategy would do. I wanted to make tax reform the defining issue of the next presidential campaign. If a serious flat-tax bill were put before Congress, I was sure the people would respond.

There would be ferocious opposition from the establishment, but so much the better. All the counterattacks I have described—warnings of national ruin from critics, fabricated statistics, bogus flat-tax alternatives—I expected from the start. But it was time to draw the lines. The idea is revolutionary, but so is the spirit of the American taxpayer. There is no modest, quiet way to scrap the tax code and free taxpayers from their burdens.

There's a timing to these things, and back in 1994 all my instincts told me the time was about to come for the flat tax. But first I had to lay the groundwork.

I remember being urged by supporters to include the flat tax in the "Contract with America." In 1994, Newt Gingrich and I, joined by our comrades-in-arms in the House, had gotten together to frame the Contract.

Amid the excitement of the occasion, some colleagues argued that the flat tax should be made part of the Contract.

I knew, however, that as a strategic and practical matter the moment had not quite come. For one thing, it was unrealistic. In the Contract, we were drawing up plans for the first hundred days of the new Congress. So monumental a reform as the flat tax could not be accomplished in one hundred days.

What became the Armey flat-tax bill had already waited a while even before I introduced it in June 1994. The flat-tax idea had been familiar to me since I first began studying economics. I read up on it again later when I taught economics in college. The idea had always attracted me, but as a professor, I couldn't do much about it, except maybe write a monograph no one but a few fellow economists would read.

Then, in 1984, I got elected to Congress. To this day I believe President Reagan was one of the greatest forces for good our country has ever seen. I was proud to be one of the foot soldiers in his cause. But the cause was only to lower taxes—not reform the system and lay waste to the tax code itself.

Actually, Reagan did consider proposing the flat tax. Apparently the idea was suggested to him by then–cabinet member George Shultz in 1982, according to Birnbaum and Murray in their book *Showdown at Gucci Gulch*:

> That same year, Secretary of State George Shultz, a former Chicago economist who was intrigued by the "flat tax" proposals of economists Robert Hall and Alvin Rabushka, tried to interest the president in the idea. In a golf match described by former Budget Director David Stockman in his book *The Triumph of Politics*, Shultz told the president that a low-rate system would end the inefficiency caused by tax loopholes and cause the economy to grow faster. By the eighteenth hole, the president was convinced, Stockman writes, and soon, "everyone around the White House was talking flat tax."

> After the golf match, then–Treasury Secretary [Donald] Regan received a short note from the president extolling the idea, scrawled in the margin of an article on the issue.

The idea, write the authors, was promptly killed by "the pragmatists in the White House." They thought "the benefits of tax reform sounded like more of the supply-siders' 'voodoo economics.'" Instead they went to work on a tax increase. One of these "pragmatists" mentioned by Birnbaum and Murray, Richard Darman, would go on to become the voice for pragmatism in the Bush White House, helping to craft the tax increase that broke Mr. Bush's "Read my lips, no new taxes" pledge of 1988.

In a sense, the flat-tax movement has had no better allies than the pragmatists in government. They have never failed us: Each time the voters demanded tax reform, the pragmatists have come through with a tax increase. The tax hike of 1990 gave us the defeat of George Bush in 1992, which gave us Bill Clinton and his own promised "middle-class tax cut." Safely in office, President Clinton and his own pragmatists quickly got to work on the tax increase of 1993. With help from still more pragmatists in Congress, the tax bill was signed into law.

Each time, I felt, the American people were growing a little more impatient with tax reform. Gradually it was becoming clear that it was not a job for pragmatists. It was after the Clinton tax hike that I first began working on a flat-tax bill.

From the get go, I wanted a bill that was both realistic and radical. I thought of the bill as a way of yanking the whole tax debate in America away from the half measures we were always proposing and weighing, modifying and watering down, and eventually discarding in Congress. I wanted a bill dramatic enough to capture the imagination of the people but restrained enough to gain a majority in Congress.

I assumed that certain deductions would have to be preserved. I knew that the question of withholding—a practice I have always considered insidious because the earner never even sees the money, it's just taken away by some invisible hand—would have to wait for another day. In my first few drafts of the bill, the mortgage and charitable deductions were left untouched.

But the more things I kept, the more my own "radical" bill began to resemble all the other tax reforms I had seen come and go. I was succumbing to the pragmatist temptation. And I'd seen where that leads.

Snapping out of that trance, I called on Rabushka and Hall about their flat-tax plan. Emphasis should go on the word *plan*: Before these two men came along, the flat tax had been little more than an abstraction. It was a beautiful thing wafting around in the ether, but without any concrete existence. Hall and Rabushka were the first to actually run the numbers, to pin the idea down and prove it actually could be done.

In its essentials, their plan became the Armey flat-tax bill, and later Armey-Shelby. My staff and I spent more months working out the finer details, and by June 1994 we were ready to go.

With that, the flat-tax idea became a bill—a real-life proposal before the Congress of the United States. Soon afterward I hit the talk-radio circuit. I wanted to take my case to the people outside the Beltway and let my colleagues in Congress hear about it from back home. To this day I don't think I have ever initiated a conversation about the flat tax with my colleagues. After hearing from their constituents, they always approached me first. I then outlined the idea in a column for a national newspaper. For days afterward, sacks of mail poured in from around the country.

Clearly, the American people—people from all parties, all regions, all stations in life—were ready. My bill was just bold enough to galvanize a public weary of timid reforms, and just realistic enough to get the job done.

Steve Forbes

When the 1996 campaign rolled around, the pundits were astonished to see the flat-tax issue catching on. I was not in the least surprised, nor would anyone who had followed me around from radio station to radio station, and from town hall to town hall. The current campaign simply marks the first time any Republican presidential candidate has offered a specific flat-tax plan to the voters. What did surprise me was the response of my Republican friends to the Steve Forbes candidacy: "He's just trying to save his own money from taxes! He's *rich*—what does he know about the lives of working people? He's just looking out for his country-club friends and that big yacht of his!"

So went the flat-tax debate back in New Hampshire. But that response had more to do with the pressures of the campaign than with the merits of the flat tax. It was a case of killing the message in order to shoot the messenger. It was also unfair to the man. I thought it took a lot of backbone for him to get out there and lay himself on the line. And if Forbes was in the race only to protect his own income, he sure chose an odd way of going about it. He could have supported someone else and saved himself $25 million in expenses, or whatever the final tab comes to.

My own take on the early primary season was a little different. It struck me as evidence of the power of the flat-tax idea that people—as every poll suggested—responded to it despite the obvious differences between themselves and the messenger. They were willing to overlook the man's wealth because of his obvious idealism, because the whole idea of the flat tax is to restore fairness and equality to our tax system. The idea is based on principles that can be understood and shared by all of us—rich, poor, or in between—principles of fairness that, in fact, unify Americans instead of driving us further apart, as previous so-called tax reforms have done.

Most people don't care much whether the messenger rides in on a helicopter, a van, or a truck: A good message is a good message. Whether you're Steve Forbes, Jerry Brown, Pat Buchanan, or Bob Dole—take the flat tax before the people, and suddenly you're going to find yourself in contention.

Lamar Alexander

More interesting than the differences over the flat tax, in any event, is the level of agreement among the surviving candidates in the 1996 campaign. When one of them, former governor Lamar Alexander, in the heat of debate, called it "a nutty idea," it fell to me to remind Lamar that the idea is wildly popular in the party he hopes to lead. I further reminded him that, according to all the polls, anywhere from 60 to 75 percent of the people of America favor the flat tax in principle. Apparently he's still against the flat tax, but I haven't heard him dismiss it as "nutty" lately. In fact, now he supports a flatter tax.

Pat Buchanan

Then there's Pat Buchanan. He's for a flat tax, with certain exemptions like the mortgage and charitable contributions deductions (although he's also for a tax on families choosing freely to buy something made in another country). When Steve Forbes jumped into contention, borne by interest in the flat tax, Pat joined in the general savaging on the grounds that without those deductions a flat tax wouldn't be fair. I intend to remind him of a column he wrote praising the "sweep and boldness" of my flat tax. Buchanan wrote that I had mapped out "the strategy for a war on Washington designed to catch the anti-Washington wave rolling across America."

The column ended with a stirring call to take on the establishment, without compromise. "Dick Armey's bold call for a flat tax, tied to an iron lid on federal spending and a rollback of state power, is a sign that the battle of ideas has been reengaged—inside the Republican party."

He didn't qualify his enthusiasm at the time with any reservations about the deductions, though, to be fair, he didn't write that he favored eliminating all deductions either. In any case, Pat is still for a flat tax, even to the point of charging that Steve Forbes had merely lifted *his* own ideas and heightened the issue with a better bankrolled campaign.

Bob Dole

As for my friend Senator Dole, despite his differences with Forbes, his flat-tax views are perhaps the most encouraging of all.

So far the Senator's most thorough statement on tax reform is an address he delivered in Chicago in the fall of 1995. "If we are to truly release all the hidden potential of this nation," he told the Chicago Economic Club, "I believe we must scrap the current tax code and start again from scratch.... The problems of today's tax code are clear," he continued.

> The top rate now stands at almost 40 percent. High marginal rates discourage work, reduce the rewards of entrepreneurship, and encourage tax avoidance. Middle-class families are forced to work harder and harder just to keep up—their hopes for a better life taxed away from government. The complexity of the code wastes billions of hours in

compliance effort and—worst of all—convinced many Americans that the tax system has been hijacked by special interests. . . .

Senator Dole went on to make at least as forceful a case for the flat tax as I have ever been able to make:

First, we need a new tax code that moves us toward a system with lower and flatter rates. During much of the past century, tax policy has been a primary tool with which government has wielded power, fed the bureaucracy, and redistributed wealth. . . . Any fair system would not penalize, but instead reward people for working harder. . . . A fair system would relieve the burden on working families. A family of four—earning up to $25,000 to $30,000 per year—should pay little or no federal income tax. . . . And a fair system would stop taxing capital twice: first as income and then as capital gains, reducing the return on risk-taking and investment.

In the same speech, Senator Dole urged passage of a constitutional amendment requiring a two-thirds majority in Congress to raise income tax rates. This, he explained, would "ensure that Congress doesn't turn a flatter tax system into a political football."

The Kemp Report

Finally, there's the recent report of the Kemp Commission on Tax Reform, about which all the candidates have spoken quite favorably. Along with Speaker Gingrich, Senator Dole in fact commissioned the report to make recommendations for the country's future. The result was a report I could have written, setting forth the same principles I relied upon in Armey-Shelby: fairness, economic growth, simplicity, stability, neutrality, and visibility.

"A single rate is a fair rate," said the report in endorsing the flat tax. "One rate, coupled with a generous personal exemption, together produce a progressive average tax rate. Low-income taxpayers would owe little or no tax. But everyone who earns enough to cross the threshold of the exemption would face exactly the same tax rate on any additional income."

The Kemp Report, hailed by all the candidates, is today the central document in tax reform debate among Republicans. It strongly urges a flat tax. It's a good bet the report will become the tax reform plank in the 1996 convention platform, whoever the nominee might be.

All in all, we've come a long way since June of 1994 when I put forward my bill to scrap the tax code and restore freedom and fairness to the American economy. Back then, we were still the minority party; tax reformers were on the defensive; the latest tax hike had come through and we were a little demoralized.

What a different world it is today! Today, Republicans are no longer playing anvil to the Democrats' hammer. And Democrats themselves are divided on the tax issue: They, too, are feeling the heat. Some, like my colleague Dick Gephardt, have responded with flimsy flat-tax plans of their own. And others, like Senator Shelby himself, who recently crossed the aisle to become a Republican, have signed on to the flat-tax movement. No matter whom he faces in the fall, President Clinton is going to find himself on the business end of the flat-tax juggernaut, and will have to explain why he opposes all-out reform of the tax code.

Differences remain in my party, but they are differences in detail. On the basic principles we're united. The pragmatists have been put to rout. Driving the debate today are the taxpayers of America, who have waited long enough for serious reform. I believe the flat tax will become law within a year—eighteen months on the outside. We're almost there, and the wind is at our backs.

A Picture of Freedom

Watching C-SPAN the other day, I heard a man in New Hampshire get right to the heart of the tax issue. In the back of the room he rose to offer a comment to one of the Republican candidates. He had worked, I believe, at a nearby factory for five years. Before that he'd been laid off from his previous job. He and his wife had two children and were now making what seemed to him pretty good money. But the taxes—he listed all the taxes he had paid in the last year—just never ended. After state, local, and federal, it came to nearly half his total earnings.

"Look," he said, "I don't mind paying my fair share in taxes. I'm proud to pay my taxes. But I can't afford to pay almost *half* my income to government. It's *my money!*"

A lot of us have felt that way lately. It *is* our money, and we should not feel apologetic about saying it. We shouldn't have to say it at all.

It is now common in our tax debates to hear people heatedly arguing whether government can or cannot "afford" to cut taxes. Economists and reporters routinely speak of how much a flat-tax rate, and the budget cuts provided for in Armey-Shelby, would "cost" the government. If leaving people with more of their own money would *cost* the government too much, as this reasoning goes, then the whole idea is out of the question.

Let's end by taking on this argument and its whole way of framing the tax issue. After all, no government in history ever bore the cost of anything. Governments do not pay for things; the people pay for government. Always, therefore, the question is what the people can afford to pay in taxes.

Among its other virtues, the flat tax will take us back to basic principles. Under today's code, the overriding issue always seems to be what government needs. If it needs more money for programs X, Y, and Z, then it's just taken as a given that the taxpayers have a duty to come up with the cash.

Built into the code are all kinds of devices to assure that it keeps coming even without our direct consent. "Bracket creep," which assures we pay higher rates the moment we earn more money, is just one of them.

A fair and rational tax system would begin with the assumption that, prior to all claims by government, wealth belongs to the earners. The wealth of America is not just the national wealth. It isn't just the GDP. It doesn't belong to "the people," but just to people. Our national wealth is made up of dollars earned, often at great sacrifice and labor, by individual people, with individual plans, hopes, and responsibilities of their own.

Though a lot of folks in Washington think government "needs" a third or half our earnings, this perceived "need" does not give them a right to take it. It's legal; it's all right there in the tax code. Look it up. But to take that much isn't *right*. It isn't fair to the people earning the money.

"Without justice," a philosopher asked long ago, "what are kingdoms but great bands of robbers?" Today we know the same question applies to democratic governments. Guiding all governments, there has to be a fixed standard; one single, solid, inviolable line between the state and the individual. We've tried running our federal government for most of this century without that standard, and this is where it's left us: paying ever-larger portions of our earnings, with no guarantee the tax bill won't get higher.

The current *Reader's Digest*—February 1996—carries a remarkable survey called "How Fair Are Our Taxes?"

"The maximum burden that Americans think a family of four should bear," according to the poll, "is 25 percent of its income. That's not just federal income tax. That's 25 percent for all major levies combined—federal, state, and local—including income, Social Security, sales, and property taxes. In fact, most Americans pay far more than this maximum."

The poll, moreover, found little of the class resentment that advocates of the current tax code are always trying to dredge up. Respondents were asked, "What is the highest percentage you think would be fair for a family making $200,000 a year to pay when you add all their taxes together?"

Answer: 25 percent. "Despite the oft-heard belief that the poor and middle class resent 'the privileged,' " according to *Reader's Digest*, "Americans earning less than $30,000 per year agreed with the other income groups that 25 percent was the maximum tax burden that would be fair for a family of four earning $200,000 a year."

"To a remarkable degree," concludes the article, "different groups of Americans agree they themselves pay too much in taxes. The percentage is the same for men and women (68 percent), virtually the same for blacks and whites (70 percent and 68 percent), conservatives and liberals (68 percent and 67 percent). By party, Republicans (73 percent) and Independents (71 percent) think their taxes are too high; even 60 percent of Democrats thinks so."

Doubtless this latter statistic would be dismissed by some as of little significance: *Of course* people think they're overtaxed, runs this objection. Whoever thought he was *under*taxed? But, while paying taxes is never pleasant, it is our civic duty and we must resist the voices of greed clamoring for lower taxes.

I've heard this one a lot during the flat-tax debate. In Washington, the flat-tax cause is nervously brushed off as just another rumbling from "out there" against the federal government. It's "antigovernment." It would have us abandon the needy, disregard our most fundamental duties, give free rein to our baser instincts, and of course let the rich off scot-free while people are living in the streets.

What always strikes me as odd about these charges, made by self-styled champions of the common man, is the low opinion they reflect of people in general. Even while appealing to our sense of idealism, they fault the common run of humanity with being greedy self-seekers who need government to prick their consciences.

Just the other night, for instance, I heard—again on TV—a voice for the other view of taxation and government. It was former New York governor Mario Cuomo, on a program called *The Open Mind*, going on and on about Speaker Newt Gingrich and the Republican Congress: the selfishness of people who think they're overtaxed, our mean-spirited disregard of the poor, our incivility.

This was followed by his usual uplifting lecture on America as one big family, our lost sense of community, our need for civility, etc., etc.

A decade or so ago, *maybe* one could sit through a Cuomo lecture on governance without laughing out loud at the absurdity of it all. I think it was his bit about civility that set me off. Who else could speak of political opponents as coldhearted degenerates in one breath and call for civility in the next?

Like so much of the old class-war rhetoric, it rings more hollow with every passing year. Just hearing him talk about the poor versus the rich, the worker versus the moneymen, the compassionate elite versus the hard-hearted reactionaries, was a nostalgic experience.

We'll be hearing these scoldings about our greed right up until the day the flat tax is signed into law, as I believe it will be—and probably for a while after that. But I believe they are the last gasps of a passing order.

After all, it's not as if we haven't tried the governor's own big-spending solutions to our problems. It's not like we need to wait a few more generations before the results come in. We've tried, all right.

Just look at New York. A great place, but I was there a few times during the governor's twelve-year tenure and did not notice any appreciable rise in civility. I did not notice a deeper sense of family and community. What I did notice was a government constantly on the brink of bankruptcy, a state and city harassed by higher crime rates and higher taxes than any other place on the North American continent. The people noticed, too. And not just in New York.

Look at the federal government: Why can't Washington afford more tax cuts? Why would a flat tax, as some see it, simply cost the government too much? Because it is already operating on a budget of $1.5 trillion—and still deeply in debt. That comes to $5,030 the government is spending for every man, woman, and child in America. From another angle, that's $24,000 for every household in America.

If we don't get control of things, by current projections the budget will be $1.8 trillion by the year 2000. By the year 2010—it will be $2.5 trillion. By the year 2020—$4 trillion.

Even if federal taxes were to rise to 25 percent of gross domestic product, the deficit (in 1990 dollars) will rise to over $300 billion in 2000; $600 billion in 2010; $1.4 trillion in 2020. How bad is the national debt today? Every child born in America today begins with a $13,000 share of our national debt.

These are the fruits of forty years' experience with big

government—forty years' worth of inspiring lectures and speeches about all the wonders big government could do for us. We could point to some modest successes here and there—people who were truly helped, a handful of programs that worked some tangible good in our lives. Some of them we may well want to keep.

But in general, most of us agree it's time to call off the grand experiment and keep more money in the hands of the earners. We tried. But two generations and $5 trillion later—the verdict is in. Good intentions alone, we now know, do not make for Great Societies. Enough reckless spending; time to put our finances in order. Enough massive social programs; we've learned from unhappy experience that every social ill cannot be solved with a check from Washington, and that private virtue works a lot better than any public program.

And enough bureaucrats: 19,800,000 people on the public payroll is too many. Enough social engineering and meddling; better to let people make their own decisions. The age of the state planner, managing our lives from afar, is behind us. Perhaps it was suited to challenges of the day: Big government and our modern tax code came into being in times of war. But today, in peace, our whole society and economy are moving in the other direction. Technology is liberating us from the whole archaic model of centralized planning. More people are working for themselves. Millions of others will soon follow. All the information once available to only a few can now be accessed by any one of us sitting at home working on a computer.

Those who would cling to our current tax code, and all the powers of social engineering it confers upon big government, are clinging in vain. All the currents of history are working against them. In modern technology and throughout our entire economy, power is rippling back out to the people. "The era of big government is over," as the president himself said recently in his State of the Union message. But it isn't over because he declared it so. It's over because it's over—because history has passed it by. One of the older clichés of the left is today turning on them: You can't turn back the clock.

"I am a registered Independent," says a supporter from Pittsburgh, "and would vote in a second for any candidate of either party running on these ideas [the flat tax]. There are probably untold millions of voters just as fed up with the government as I am who would do the same."

"I am a Democrat," writes a man from Bristol, Tennessee. "I am also an African-American. I am writing in support of your proposal for a flat tax. My wife and I are sick of the present mess that is supposed to be a fair and simple tax system."

"Although I consider myself a Democrat," says a woman from Davenport, Iowa, "I agree with you 100 percent and support your ideas. I do not see any other fair method of taxation. I believe the current system is entirely unjust. I cannot see the fairness in charging some people a certain tax percentage and others a higher percentage. I don't understand why there are so many deductions that only the elite can afford to take."

None of these are "antigovernment" sentiments. I do not sense any of the class consciousness that critics of the flat tax are trying to stir up.

As I read them, they are just simple calls for good government by people who ask only to manage their own lives and bear their own responsibilities. That's another side of today's freedom revolution: As a country, even as technology changes our economic landscape, we seem to have concluded that the Founders were on to a pretty good idea over two centuries ago: The best government is limited government.

We are a community, and we do have obligations to one another, but those, too, are *ours*. They cannot be shifted onto the state. I believe in the duties of community and charity as

117

much, I think, as Mario Cuomo—I just don't believe in turning them over to him or to the state. Charity and love work better as private virtues than government programs. A diffuse, sentimental vision of "social responsibility" makes a poor substitute for personal responsibility. There's no surer way to kill human compassion than to make it compulsory.

The idea of limited government isn't that we can all just walk away from people in need, from our duties to our neighbors. The idea is that those are all individual callings. Most responsibilities we undertake in life—marriage, parenthood, vocation—are personal. They have little or nothing to do with the state. They're ours alone, freely accepted. In fact, only by doing them ourselves do we come to realize that they're not burdens at all.

As for the letter writer's feeling of being "fed-up with government," I don't think the folks in Washington need worry too much about that. The Republic will survive. All the man is saying is that there are too many bureaucrats and they're getting a little too aggressive. Most of us know exactly what he means. Most of us also know some pretty good public servants, too. The problem is that, like us, they find themselves within a system fundamentally unmanageable. They want good government as much as we do. They just don't know where to begin.

The answer lies with the tax code. It was the idea of graduated rates that first set in motion so many of the problems, the abuses of power, the corruption and special preferences taxpayers today find so unfair. With one bill—one law—we can begin setting things right again. We'll pay less in taxes, and in return we'll get better government. We'll each pay at the same rate, and we'll each keep and earn more. One new law will replace a thousand old and outdated ones, one standard of fairness for all Americans, one bold stroke for freedom.

So many things turn on this one reform. Change the tax code, and we'll have changed the world. Nothing we could do, no other political reform, would more surely improve our own lives or the lives of our neighbors.

Frequently Asked Questions

Will your flat-tax plan increase the deficit?

Absolutely not. My plan will allow us to eliminate the deficit and achieve a balanced budget within seven years—exactly as Congress currently plans.

Let me be clear. The proposal will initially collect less revenue for the government than the current tax system. But this revenue loss will be no more than $20 billion to $40 billion in the first year, out of a $1.5 trillion federal budget. We can easily make up this shortfall with modest spending cuts. And compliance costs will drop dramatically.

You may hear wild charges that the flat tax will expand the deficit, but these charges are based on discredited and usually dishonest studies (see chapter 10).

Is the flat tax progressive?

Sure it is. Because of the generous family allowances—which exempt the first $33,300 of income for a family of four—middle-income people pay a far lower share of their income in taxes than the rich do, and the poor pay nothing at all. Think about it. If a family of four makes $50,000 a year, the 17 percent flat-tax rate applies to less than half of that family's income. But if a family of four makes $200,000, the 17 percent flat-tax rate applies to over 80 percent of that family's income.

But even if that flat tax didn't have this progressive feature, the rich would still pay a lot more in taxes than the middle class or the poor. With three times the net income (after taking out your personal exemptions), you pay three times the taxes. Ten times the net income, ten times the taxes. And so on. That seems pretty fair to me.

Will the family allowance be indexed for inflation?

Yes.

I've heard the flat tax will increase taxes on the middle class. Is that true?

No. Americans at all income levels will have their taxes reduced. Not only will taxpayers keep more of their money, but their incomes will increase. Under the flat tax, the typical family will see its income rise by $5,000 to $7,000 within five years.

How can I be sure that politicians won't try to raise the rate above 17 percent?

Two reasons. Because the flat tax treats all taxpayers the same, we will all be united against any tax increase. The days are over when the politicians could divide us by raising taxes on some of us (only to get the rest later).

Second, as a special safeguard, my bill requires a three-fifths super-majority vote of *both* the House and Senate before the tax rate could be raised or the level of family allowance lowered.

Would you also need a super-majority to *lower* the 17 percent rate?

Nope. A simple majority will suffice to lower the rate from 17 percent.

I've heard that the flat tax doesn't tax investors' income. Is this true?

No, that's flat wrong. The flat tax taxes all income at the same 17 percent rate, whether it comes from wages, stock dividends, or some other source.

Again, here's how it works. There are two tax forms—one applies to personal income (defined as wages, salaries, and pensions) and the other applies to business income (everything else). Typically, the business form will be filled out by corporations and other businesses, which will then make a tax payment directly to the government. That means that when an investor receives a stock dividend, he will not pay taxes on it—*because the taxes have already been paid by the business giving the dividend.*

Why do you tax this income at the business end rather than when the individual receives it?

Because it's vastly more efficient to do it that way. By taxing investment income at its source—the business itself—there's no need for the IRS enforcement bureaucracy to compare what businesses say they're earning with what individuals say they are receiving.

To keep track of this income under today's system, Americans must fill out more than *one billion* 1099 forms each year. By taxing business income at the source, these compliance costs evaporate.

Will I be able to afford my home mortgage without the mortgage interest deduction?

Yes. Every study on the flat tax shows that it will lower interest rates—and that includes studies done by flat-tax opponents. A Federal Reserve economist, for instance, recently reported that interest rates will drop 25 percent. Right now that's equal to about 2 percentage points.

This means that it will not only be easier to afford your home under the flat tax, but the housing market will prosper as well. Don't forget, you'll also be keeping more of the money you earn.

Won't charities suffer as a result of the flat tax?

No. Almost half of charitable contributions today are not even claimed as deductions, so ending the break would have no effect on that giving.

In general, charitable giving increases when Americans have more money in their pockets because of lower taxes and higher economic growth. Under the flat tax, the income of the typical family of four would increase by $5,000 to $7,000 within five years. The American people will respond to their freedom and greater prosperity as they've always done, by opening their hearts and their wallets to their neighbors.

I've been deducting business expenses that I personally pay for—like transportation, subscriptions, a computer. How will these expenses be affected by a flat tax?

Under the flat tax, you will still enjoy these legitimate deductions, which would be listed on the business form.

How will the flat tax affect pensions, 401Ks, and other retirement plans?

Because the flat tax ends the bias against saving, in effect all income that is saved will be treated like an IRA or a pension. Currently, IRAs, 401(k)s, and pensions are unusual because they are taxed only once. Under the flat tax, *all* savings will be taxed only once. That will make it easier for Americans to save for their children's education, their own retirement, or anything else.

How will state and local governments be affected by a flat tax?

State and local governments will benefit from the high-growth economy, which will pour more revenue into their treasuries.

Further, tax reform in Washington might very well lead to tax reform at the state and local level, too. The flat tax could set in motion a chain of reform affecting government at all levels. There would be pressure on state governments to enact flat taxes of their own.

How does the flat tax affect payroll taxes, excise taxes, or other federal taxes?

The flat tax is a complete replacement of the personal, corporate, estate, and gift taxes. It would leave all other federal taxes untouched.

When can we expect the flat tax to pass?

A lot depends on the 1996 election. I have no doubt if the candidate elected in November is committed to tax reform, we'll see a flat-tax bill signed into law in 1997.

Appendix

Note: The personal exemption levels in the following bill apply to the first year of the flat tax. By the third year, when the flat tax is fully phased in, the personal exemption for a family of four is $33,300. It is indexed for inflation.

104TH CONGRESS
1ST SESSION

H. R. 2060

To promote freedom, fairness, and economic opportunity for families by
reducing the power and reach of the Federal establishment.

IN THE HOUSE OF REPRESENTATIVES

JULY 19, 1995

Mr. ARMEY introduced the following bill; which was referred to the Committee
on Ways and Means, and in addition to the Committees on Government
Reform and Oversight, the Budget, and Rules, for a period to be subse-
quently determined by the Speaker, in each case for consideration of such
provisions as fall within the jurisdiction of the committee concerned

---

A BILL

To promote freedom, fairness, and economic opportunity for
families by reducing the power and reach of the Federal
establishment.

1   *Be it enacted by the Senate and House of Representa-*
2   *tives of the United States of America in Congress assembled,*
3   **SECTION 1. SHORT TITLE.**
4   (a) SHORT TITLE.—This Act may be cited as the
5   "Freedom and Fairness Restoration Act of 1995".
6   (b) TABLE OF CONTENTS.—

Sec. 1. Short title.

TITLE I—TAX REDUCTION AND SIMPLIFICATION;
SUPERMAJORITY REQUIRED FOR TAX CHANGES

129

2

•HR 2060 IH

3

1 **TITLE I—TAX REDUCTION AND**
2 **SIMPLIFICATION;**
3 **SUPERMAJORITY REQUIRED**
4 **FOR TAX CHANGES**
5 **Subtitle A—Tax Reduction and**
6 **Simplification**

7 SEC. 101. INDIVIDUAL INCOME TAX.

8   (a) IN GENERAL.—Section 1 of the Internal Revenue
9 Code of 1986 is amended to read as follows:

10 "SECTION 1. TAX IMPOSED.

11   "There is hereby imposed on the taxable income of
12 every individual a tax equal to 20 percent (17 percent in
13 the case of taxable years beginning after December 31,
14 1997) of the taxable income of such individual for such
15 taxable year."

16   (b) TAXABLE INCOME.—Section 63 of such Code is
17 amended to read as follows:

18 "SEC. 63. TAXABLE INCOME.

19   "(a) IN GENERAL.—For purposes of this subtitle, the
20 term 'taxable income' means the excess of—

21   "(1) the sum of—

22   "(A) wages (as defined in section 3121(a)

23   without regard to paragraph (1) thereof) which

24   are paid in cash and which are received during

4

1   the taxable year for services performed in the

2   United States,

3   "(B) retirement distributions which are in-

4   cludible in gross income for such taxable year,

5   plus

6   "(C) amounts received under any law of

7   the United States or of any State which is in

8   the nature of unemployment compensation, over

9   "(2) the standard deduction.

10   "(b) STANDARD DEDUCTION.—

11   "(1) IN GENERAL.—For purposes of this sub-

12   title, the term 'standard deduction' means the sum

13   of—

14   "(A) the basic standard deduction, plus

15   "(B) the additional standard deduction.

16   "(2) BASIC STANDARD DEDUCTION.—For pur-

17   poses of paragraph (1), the basic standard deduction

18   is—

19   "(A) $21,400 in the case of—

20   "(i) a joint return, or

21   "(ii) a surviving spouse (as defined in

22   section 2(a)),

23   "(B) $14,000 in the case of a head of

24   household (as defined in section 2(b)), and

5

1   "(C) $10,700 in the case of an individ-
2   ual—

3   "(i) who is not married and who is
4   not a surviving spouse or head of house-
5   hold, or

6   "(ii) who is a married individual filing
7   a separate return.

8   "(3) ADDITIONAL STANDARD DEDUCTION.—For
9   purposes of paragraph (1), the additional standard
10 deduction is $5,000 for each dependent (as defined
11 in section 152) who is described in section 151(c)(1)
12 for the taxable year and who is not required to file
13 a return for such taxable year.

14 "(c) RETIREMENT DISTRIBUTIONS.—For purposes of
15 subsection (a), the term 'retirement distribution' means
16 any distribution from—

17   "(1) a plan described in section 401(a) which
18   includes a trust exempt from tax under section
19   501(a),

20   "(2) an annuity plan described in section
21   403(a),

22   "(3) an annuity contract described in section
23   403(b),

24   "(4) an individual retirement account described
25   in section 408(a),

6

1   "(5) an individual retirement annuity described

2   in section 408(b),

3   "(6) an eligible deferred compensation plan (as

4   defined in section 457);

5   "(7) a governmental plan (as defined in section

6   414(d)); or

7   "(8) a trust described in section 501(c)(18).

8 Such term includes any plan, contract, account, annuity,

9 or trust which, at any time, has been determined by the

10 Secretary to be such a plan, contract, account, annuity,

11 or trust.

12   "(d) INCOME OF CERTAIN CHILDREN.—For purposes

13 of this subtitle—

14   "(1) an individual's taxable income shall include

15   the taxable income of each dependent child of such

16   individual who has not attained age 14 as of the

17   close of such taxable year, and

18   "(2) such dependent child shall have no liability

19   for tax imposed by section 1 with respect to such in-

20   come and shall not be required to file a return for

21   such taxable year.

22   "(e) INFLATION ADJUSTMENT.—

23   "(1) IN GENERAL.—In the case of any taxable

24   year beginning in a calendar year after 1996, each

25   dollar amount contained in subsection (b) shall be

•HR 2060 IH

7

1 increased by an amount determined by the Secretary

2 to be equal to—

3   "(A) such dollar amount, multiplied by

4   "(B) the cost-of-living adjustment for such

5   calendar year.

6   "(2) COST-OF-LIVING ADJUSTMENT.—For pur-

7 poses of paragraph (1), the cost-of-living adjustment

8 for any calendar year is the percentage (if any) by

9 which—

10   "(A) the CPI for the preceding calendar

11   year, exceeds

12   "(B) the CPI for the calendar year 1995.

13   "(3) CPI FOR ANY CALENDAR YEAR.—For pur-

14 poses of paragraph (2), the CPI for any calendar

15 year is the average of the Consumer Price Index as

16 of the close of the 12-month period ending on Au-

17 gust 31 of such calendar year.

18   "(4) CONSUMER PRICE INDEX.—For purposes

19 of paragraph (3), the term 'Consumer Price Index'

20 means the last Consumer Price Index for all-urban

21 consumers published by the Department of Labor.

22 For purposes of the preceding sentence, the revision

23 of the Consumer Price Index which is most consist-

24 ent with the Consumer Price Index for calendar year

25 1986 shall be used.

8

1   "(5) ROUNDING.—If any increase determined
2   under paragraph (1) is not a multiple of $10, such
3   increase shall be rounded to the next highest mul-
4   tiple of $10.

5   "(f) MARITAL STATUS.—For purposes of this section,
6 marital status shall be determined under section 7703."

7 **SEC. 102. TAX ON BUSINESS ACTIVITIES.**

8   (a) IN GENERAL.—Section 11 of the Internal Reve-
9 nue Code of 1986 (relating to tax imposed on corpora-
10 tions) is amended to read as follows:

11 **"SEC. 11. TAX IMPOSED ON BUSINESS ACTIVITIES.**

12   "(a) TAX IMPOSED.—There is hereby imposed on
13 every person engaged in a business activity a tax equal
14 to 20 percent (17 percent in the case of taxable years be-
15 ginning after December 31, 1997) of the business taxable
16 income of such person.

17   "(b) LIABILITY FOR TAX.—The tax imposed by this
18 section shall be paid by the person engaged in the business
19 activity, whether such person is an individual, partnership,
20 corporation, or otherwise.

21   "(c) BUSINESS TAXABLE INCOME.—For purposes of
22 this section—

23   "(1) IN GENERAL.—The term 'business taxable
24   income' means gross active income reduced by the
25   deductions specified in subsection (d).

9

1   "(2) GROSS ACTIVE INCOME.—

2   "(A) IN GENERAL.—For purposes of para-

3   graph (1), the term 'gross active income' means

4   gross receipts from—

5   "(i) the sale or exchange of property

6   or services in the United States by any

7   person in connection with a business activ-

8   ity, and

9   "(ii) the export of property or services

10   from the United States in connection with

11   a business activity.

12   "(B) EXCHANGES.—For purposes of this

13   section, the amount treated as gross receipts

14   from the exchange of property or services is the

15   fair market value of the property or services re-

16   ceivod, plus any money received.

17   "(C) COORDINATION WITH SPECIAL RULES

18   FOR FINANCIAL SERVICES, ETC.—Except as

19   provided in subsection (e)—

20   "(i) the term 'property' does not in-

21   clude money or any financial instrument,

22   and

23   "(ii) the term 'services' does not in-

24   clude financial services.

HR 2060 IH——2

10

"(3) EXEMPTION FROM TAX FOR ACTIVITIES OF GOVERNMENTAL ENTITIES AND TAX-EXEMPT ORGANIZATIONS.—For purposes of this section, the term 'business activity' does not include any activity of a governmental entity or of any other organization which is exempt from tax under this chapter.

"(d) DEDUCTIONS.—

"(1) IN GENERAL.—The deductions specified in this subsection are—

"(A) the cost of business inputs for the business activity,

"(B) wages (as defined in section 3121(a) without regard to paragraph (1) thereof) which are paid in cash for services performed in the United States as an employee, and

"(C) retirement contributions to or under any plan or arrangement which makes retirement distributions (as defined in section 63(c)) for the benefit of such employees to the extent such contributions are allowed as a deduction under section 404.

"(2) BUSINESS INPUTS.—

"(A) IN GENERAL.—For purposes of paragraph (1), the term 'cost of business inputs' means—

11

1   "(i) the amount paid for property sold

2   or used in connection with a business ac-

3   tivity,

4   "(ii) the amount paid for services

5   (other than for the services of employees,

6   including fringe benefits paid by reason of

7   such services) in connection with a busi-

8   ness activity, and

9   "(iii) any excise tax, sales tax, cus-

10   toms duty, or other separately stated levy

11   imposed by a Federal, State, or local gov-

12   ernment on the purchase of property or

13   services which are for use in connection

14   with a business activity.

15   Such term shall not include any tax imposed by

16   chapter 2 or 21.

17   "(B) EXCEPTIONS.—Such term shall not

18   include—

19   "(i) items described in subparagraphs

20   (B) and (C) of paragraph (1), and

21   "(ii) items for personal use not in

22   connection with any business activity.

23   "(C) EXCHANGES.—For purposes of this

24   section, the amount treated as paid in connec-

25   tion with the exchange of property or services

12

1   is the fair market value of the property or serv-

2   ices exchanged, plus any money paid.

3   "(e) SPECIAL RULES FOR FINANCIAL INTER-

4 MEDIATION SERVICE ACTIVITIES.—In the case of the

5 business activity of providing financial intermediation

6 services, the taxable income from such activity shall be

7 equal to the value of the intermediation services provided

8 in such activity.

9   "(f) EXCEPTION FOR SERVICES PERFORMED AS EM-

10 PLOYEE.—For purposes of this section, the term 'business

11 activity' does not include the performance of services by

12 an employee for the employee's employer.

13   "(g) CARRYOVER OF EXCESS DEDUCTIONS.—

14   "(1) IN GENERAL.—If the aggregate deductions

15   for any taxable year exceed the gross active income

16   for such taxable year, the amount of the deductions

17   specified in subsection (d) for the succeeding taxable

18   year (determined without regard to this subsection)

19   shall be increased by the sum of—

20   "(A) such excess, plus

21   "(B) the product of such excess and the 3-

22   month Treasury rate for the last month of such

23   taxable year.

24   "(2) 3-MONTH TREASURY RATE.—For purposes

25   of paragraph (1), the 3-month Treasury rate is the

13

1   rate determined by the Secretary based on the aver-

2   age market yield (during any 1-month period se-

3   lected by the Secretary and ending in the calendar

4   month in which the determination is made) on out-

5   standing marketable obligations of the United States

6   with remaining periods to maturity of 3 months or

7   less.''

8   (b) TAX ON TAX-EXEMPT ENTITIES PROVIDING

9 NONCASH COMPENSATION TO EMPLOYEES.—Section

10 4977 of such Code is amended to read as follows:

11 **"SEC. 4977. TAX ON NONCASH COMPENSATION PROVIDED**

12   **TO EMPLOYEES NOT ENGAGED IN BUSINESS**

13   **ACTIVITY.**

14   "(a) IMPOSITION OF TAX.—There is hereby imposed

15 a tax equal to 20 percent (17 percent in the case of cal-

16 endar years beginning after December 31, 1997) of the

17 value of excludable compensation provided during the cal-

18 endar year by an employer for the benefit of employees

19 to whom this section applies.

20   "(b) LIABILITY FOR TAX.—The tax imposed by this

21 section shall be paid by the employer.

22   "(c) EXCLUDABLE COMPENSATION.—For purposes

23 of subsection (a), the term 'excludable compensation'

24 means any remuneration for services performed as an em-

25 ployee other than—

•HR 2060 IH

14

1   "(1) wages (as defined in section 3121(a) with-

2   out regard to paragraph (1) thereof) which are paid

3   in cash,

4   "(2) remuneration for services performed out-

5   side the United States, and

6   "(3) retirement contributions to or under any

7   plan or arrangement which makes retirement dis-

8   tributions (as defined in section 63(c)).

9 "(d) EMPLOYEES TO WHOM SECTION APPLIES.—

10 This section shall apply to an employee who is employed

11 in any activity by—

12   "(1) any organization which is exempt from

13   taxation under this chapter, or

14   "(2) any agency or instrumentality of the

15   United States, any State or political subdivision of

16   a State, or the District of Columbia."

17 **SEC. 103. SIMPLIFICATION OF RULES RELATING TO QUALI-**

18   **FIED RETIREMENT PLANS.**

19   (a) IN GENERAL.—The following provisions of the In-

20 ternal Revenue Code of 1986 are hereby repealed:

21   (1) NONDISCRIMINATION RULES.—

22   (A) Paragraphs (4) and (5) of section

23   401(a) (relating to nondiscrimination require-

24   ments).

15

1   (B) Sections 401(a)(10)(B) and 416 (re-
2 lating to top heavy plans).

3   (C) Section 401(a)(17) (relating to com-
4 pensation limit).

5   (D) Sections 401(a)(26) and 410(b) (relat-
6 ing to minimum participation and coverage re-
7 quirements).

8   (E) Sections 401(k)(3), 401(k)(8), and
9 4979 (relating to actual deferral percentage).

10   (F) Section 401(l) (relating to permitted
11 disparity in plan contributions or benefits).

12   (G) Section 401(m) (relating to non-
13 discrimination test for matching contributions
14 and employee contributions).

15   (H) Paragraphs (1)(D) and (12) of section
16 403(b) (relating to nondiscrimination require-
17 ments).

18   (I) Paragraph (3) of section 408(k) and
19 paragraph (6) (other than subparagraph (A)(i))
20 of such section (relating to simplified employee
21 pensions).

22 (2) CONTRIBUTION LIMITS.—

23   (A) Sections 401(a)(16), 403(b) (2) and
24 (3), and 415 (relating to limitations on benefits
25 and contributions under qualified plans).

16

1   (B) Sections 401(a)(30) and 402(g) (relat-
2   ing to limitation on exclusion for elective defer-
3   rals).

4   (C) Paragraphs (3) and (7) of section
5   404(a) (relating to percentage of compensation
6   limits).

7   (D) Section 404(l) (relating to limit on in-
8   cludible compensation).

9   (3) RESTRICTIONS ON DISTRIBUTIONS.—

10   (A) Section 72(t) (relating to 10-percent
11   additional tax on early distributions from quali-
12   fied retirement plans).

13   (B) Sections 401(a)(9), 403(b)(10), and
14   4974 (relating to minimum distribution rules).

15   (C) Section 402(d) (relating to tax on
16   lump sum distributions).

17   (D) Section 402(e)(4) (relating to net un-
18   realized appreciation).

19   (E) Section 4980A (relating to tax on ex-
20   cess distributions from qualified retirement
21   plans).

22   (4) SPECIAL REQUIREMENTS FOR PLAN BENE-
23   FITING SELF-EMPLOYED INDIVIDUALS.—Subsections
24   (a)(10)(A) and (d) of section 401.

•HR 2060 IH

17

1   (5) PROHIBITION OF TAX-EXEMPT ORGANIZA-
2   TIONS AND GOVERNMENTS FROM HAVING QUALIFIED
3   CASH   OR   DEFERRED   ARRANGEMENTS.—Section
4   401(k)(4)(B).

5   (b) EMPLOYER REVERSIONS OF EXCESS PENSION
6 ASSETS PERMITTED SUBJECT ONLY TO INCOME INCLU-
7 SION.—

8   (1) REPEAL OF TAX ON EMPLOYER REVER-
9   SIONS.—Section 4980 of such Code is hereby re-
10   pealed.

11   (2) EMPLOYER REVERSIONS PERMITTED WITH-
12   OUT PLAN TERMINATION.—Section 420 of such
13   Code is amended to read as follows:

14 **"SEC. 420. TRANSFERS OF EXCESS PENSION ASSETS.**

15   "(a) IN GENERAL.—If there is a qualified transfer
16 of any excess pension assets of a defined benefit plan
17 (other than a multiemployer plan) to an employer—

18   "(1) a trust which is part of such plan shall not
19   be treated as failing to meet the requirements of sec-
20   tion 401(a) or any other provision of law solely by
21   reason of such transfer (or any other action author-
22   ized under this section), and

23   "(2) such transfer shall not be treated as a pro-
24   hibited transaction for purposes of section 4975.

HR 2060 IH——3

18

1 The gross income of the employer shall include the amount
2 of any qualified transfer made during the taxable year.

3   "(b) QUALIFIED TRANSFER.—For purposes of this
4 section—

5   "(1) IN GENERAL.—The term 'qualified trans-
6   fer' means a transfer—

7   "(A) of excess pension assets of a defined
8   benefit plan to the employer, and

9   "(B) with respect to which the vesting re-
10   quirements of subsection (c) are met in connec-
11   tion with the plan.

12   "(2) ONLY 1 TRANSFER PER YEAR.—No more
13   than 1 transfer with respect to any plan during a
14   taxable year may be treated as a qualified transfer
15   for purposes of this section.

16   "(c) VESTING REQUIREMENTS OF PLANS TRANSFER-
17 RING ASSETS.—The vesting requirements of this sub-
18 section are met if the plan provides that the accrued pen-
19 sion benefits of any participant or beneficiary under the
20 plan become nonforfeitable in the same manner which
21 would be required if the plan had terminated immediately
22 before the qualified transfer (or in the case of a partici-
23 pant who separated during the 1-year period ending on
24 the date of the transfer, immediately before such separa-
25 tion).

19

1   "(d) DEFINITION AND SPECIAL RULE.—For pur-

2 poses of this section—

3   "(1) EXCESS PENSION ASSETS.—The term 'ex-

4   cess pension assets' means the excess (if any) of—

5   "(A) the amount determined under section

6   412(c)(7)(A)(ii), over

7   "(B) the greater of—

8   "(i) the amount determined under

9   section 412(c)(7)(A)(i), or

10   "(ii) 125 percent of current liability

11   (as defined in section 412(c)(7)(B)).

12 The determination under this paragraph shall be

13 made as of the most recent valuation date of the

14 plan preceding the qualified transfer.

15   "(2) COORDINATION WITH SECTION 412.—In

16   the case of a qualified transfer—

17   "(A) any assets transferred in a plan year

18   on or before the valuation date for such year

19   (and any income allocable thereto) shall, for

20   purposes of section 412, be treated as assets in

21   the plan as of the valuation date for such year,

22   and

23   "(B) the plan shall be treated as having a

24   net experience loss under section

25   412(b)(2)(B)(iv) in an amount equal to the

20

1   amount of such transfer and for which amorti-
2   zation charges begin for the first plan year
3   after the plan year in which such transfer oc-
4   curs, except that such section shall be applied
5   to such amount by substituting '10 plan years'
6   for '5 plan years'."

7 **SEC. 104. REPEAL OF ALTERNATIVE MINIMUM TAX.**

8   Part VI of subchapter A of chapter 1 of the Internal
9 Revenue Code of 1986 is hereby repealed.

10 **SEC. 105. REPEAL OF CREDITS.**

11   Part IV of subchapter A of chapter 1 of the Internal
12 Revenue Code of 1986 is hereby repealed.

13 **SEC. 106. REPEAL OF ESTATE AND GIFT TAXES AND OBSO-**
14   **LETE INCOME TAX PROVISIONS.**

15   (a) REPEAL OF ESTATE AND GIFT TAXES.—

16   (1) IN GENERAL.—Subtitle B of the Internal
17   Revenue Code of 1986 is hereby repealed.

18   (2) EFFECTIVE DATE.—The repeal made by
19   paragraph (1) shall apply to the estates of decedents
20   dying, and gifts and generation-skipping transfers
21   made, after December 31, 1995.

22   (b) REPEAL OF OBSOLETE INCOME TAX PROVI-
23 SIONS.—

21

1   (1) IN GENERAL.—Except as provided in para-
2   graph (2), chapter 1 of the Internal Revenue Code
3   of 1986 is hereby repealed.

4   (2) EXCEPTIONS.—Paragraph (1) shall not
5   apply to—

6   (A) sections 1, 11, and 63 of such Code,
7   as amended by this Act,

8   (B) those provisions of chapter 1 of such
9   Code which are necessary for determining
10   whether or not—

11   (i) retirement distributions are includ-
12   ible in the gross income of employees, or

13   (ii) an organization is exempt from
14   tax under such chapter, and

15   (C) subchapter D of such chapter 1 (relat-
16   ing to deferred compensation).

17 **SEC. 107. EFFECTIVE DATE.**

18   Except as otherwise provided in this subtitle, the
19 amendments made by this subtitle shall apply to taxable
20 years beginning after December 31, 1995.

21 ## Subtitle B—Supermajority
22 ## Required for Tax Changes

23 **SEC. 111. SUPERMAJORITY REQUIRED.**

24   (a) IN GENERAL.—It shall not be in order in the
25 House of Representatives or the Senate to consider any

22

1 bill, joint resolution, amendment thereto, or conference re-
2 port thereon that includes any provision that—

3   (1) increases any Federal income tax rate,

4   (2) creates any additional Federal income tax
5   rate,

6   (3) reduces the standard deduction, or

7   (4) provides any exclusion, deduction, credit or
8   other benefit which results in a reduction in Federal
9   revenues.

10   (b) WAIVER OR SUSPENSION.—This section may be
11 waived or suspended in the House of Representatives or
12 the Senate only by the affirmative vote of three-fifths of
13 the Members, duly chosen and sworn.